Ready to Learn

Using Play to Build Literacy Skills in Young Learners

Anne Burke

Pembroke Publishers Limited

For little wolf Aidan,
the King of all wild things

© **2010 Pembroke Publishers**
538 Hood Road
Markham, Ontario, Canada L3R 3K9
www.pembrokepublishers.com

Distributed in the U.S. by Stenhouse Publishers
480 Congress Street
Portland, ME 04101
www.stenhouse.com

We acknowledge the financial support of the Government of Canada through the Book Publishing Industry Development Program (BPIDP) for our publishing activities.

We acknowledge the assistance of the Government of Ontario through the Ontario Media Development Corporation's Ontario Book Initiative.

Library and Archives Canada Cataloguing in Publication

Burke, Anne M. (Anne Michelle)

   Ready to learn : using play to build literacy skills
in young learners / Anne Burke.

Includes index.
ISBN 978-1-55138-249-4

1. Reading (Primary). 2. Play. 3. Problem solving. I. Title.

LB1525.B895 2010   372.4   C2009-907087-1

Editor: Kate Revington
Cover Design: John Zehethofer
Typesetting: Jay Tee Graphics Ltd.

Printed and bound in Canada
9 8 7 6 5 4 3 2 1

Mixed Sources
Product group from well-managed forests, and other controlled sources
www.fsc.org Cert no. SW-COC-002358
© 1996 Forest Stewardship Council
FSC

Contents

Foreword

On three occasions in recent memory, I was engaged in the delightful activity of "Kid-watching" — observing children at play.

The first event involved my 20-month-old granddaughter. Playing on the living-room rug with her new holiday toy, she began announcing the names of the letters appearing in random order on the illuminated face of the computer screen on the colorful plastic module. She knew the names of each letter of the alphabet, and although she has a limited speaking vocabulary, revealed great glee in speaking them aloud as they flashed on the screen, unaided by any adult instructor. She could identify every letter of the alphabet.

On the second occasion, two-year-old Liam was putting away his toys and counting each one aloud as he placed it in the toy box: "one, two, . . . twenty." The numbers were already in his head, ready to be employed at will.

The third situation concerned six-year-old Aidan, who was teaching me to play a video game that involved each of us holding a piece of gaming equipment that controlled an on-screen automobile speeding along a wildly curving road. I, of course, was unable to keep my car on the road and the car was crashing continually. Aidan whispered to me: "Don't worry, Mr. Booth. You'll improve as you play more."

All of these events feature children learning through play, experimenting, constructing, testing, repeating, remembering, evaluating, improving, making sense — all the while completely engaged in the "real" activity. In Anne Burke's approach to understanding the role of play in the learning lives of children, we come to recognize the power and necessity of this everyday process inherent in growing up; we also come to value the research and study that support the inclusion of play in the curriculum of childhood. This book, then, presents us with both the research and the practice of play. It strengthens our resolve as teachers and as parents to see play as the heart of learning for youngsters, a significant component of our definition of learning in every part of the curriculum.

I find the framework of Anne's book so helpful in presenting an overview of the contributions that play can bring to our experiences with children, incorporating so many cognitive and affective processes, and in a variety of dynamic venues. The integration of the curriculum areas becomes readily apparent as children behave as scientists, geographers, mathematicians, and readers and writers inside the constructs that teachers establish in the classroom. Children solve problems, conduct experiments, record results, dramatize stories, sing community songs, interact with technology, design a cityscape, build a cardboard castle, and role-play heroes.

Play is real work; the thinking and languaging that occur during play represent authentic learning as children confront problems, construct realities, and communicate concerns and ideas through talking, writing, and taking part in the arts.

Teachers are extremely important to these experiences — observing behaviors and attitudes, encouraging exploration of different learning modes, promoting literacy awareness, deepening responses, and strengthening peer relationships. To observe an effective teacher in a classroom where play and learning are successfully intertwined is to see education at its best: the participants are engaged in "deep learning," establishing habits of mind and patterns of behavior that are the building blocks for their futures. As the narratives and examples in this book demonstrate, the structures supporting learning through play are vital in order for a classroom to function, and preparation is the hallmark of these programs both in establishing routines and resources and in knowing the strong expectations and outcomes that a fine program would strive towards.

Anne also brings to this book an awareness of the New Literacies that these children will encounter in their lives, the digital world of meaning making and the many modes and forms of texts that will confront our youngsters as they grow — some not even thought of as yet. We want strong, secure students who will meet these changes and challenges with energy and excitement, who will interpret and construct meaning in a variety of ways: risk takers, communicators, and researchers online, in print, and in the arts. Children need to be in charge of much of their learning, ready to jump in, try out and retry, hypothesize, regroup, brainstorm together, wonder, discuss, debate, reuse, discover — all the processes we find organically in play.

I especially like the snippets of classroom life that Anne embeds in her book: these are gleaned from her school visits and conversations with teachers who understand what play can do and why play matters to child development. There are also lists of suggestions for promoting play-based learning events that can strengthen so many aspects of the daily program in primary classrooms. They all draw upon the theoretical framework that Anne has developed in her own studies about how to help children grow into literate, thoughtful, and cooperative adults.

Ready to Learn celebrates play and yet instructs us in its classroom functions and methods — we can see the holistic opportunities for learning that play enables. The book also urges us to support and encourage teachers and parents in promoting these meaningful learning experiences in their schools. Play is not a four-letter word in education; it is the heart of learning. Engagement is the true motivator for learning, and play, we know, does this from the inside out.

Thanks, Anne.

David Booth
Professor
OISE/University of Toronto
and Nipissing University

1

Using Play to Build Literacy Foundations

Through their earliest years of play, children develop a substantial body of skills and knowledge which they bring to the classroom when they first enter a school. Most of them vaguely realize that attending school means they will learn to read and write, make new friends, and take their first real steps towards independence. They will do this on the foundations of what they already know.

One of the biggest challenges that face educators is how to reconcile this early childhood knowledge with the formal education experience. A significant part of the early years' school curriculum is finding ways to build a base of knowledge on which skills may be taught. Programs, therefore, need to be designed in such a way that they address the needs of all children but are constructed in a manner that reflects the best knowledge and practices by which children learn.

Play as a Social Activity

This book is about play and the way play can interact with early educational experiences. Pioneering psychologist Lev Vygotsky described *social play* as the way in which children come to understand rules, and just as important, that there are rules that underlie all their social interactions. All children's actions take on symbolic meaning, and through play, children build understanding of the world around them. Play is inherently social, and it facilitates children's integration into peer groups and collaborative learning spaces. It is needed for children to assume other roles and viewpoints, and to establish close interpersonal communication. In other words, play and children's social interactions are irrevocably linked. As educators, we must understand that children do best when their social interactions are valued in the learning experience.

"I play more with friends who are in school than out of school as other kids are at clubs a lot. If you knock on the door and they are not there I get a bit bored."

"At school you can play with friends. I don't have friends after school."

— Children quoted in the 2009 British Playday study (coordinated by Play England)

Of the children surveyed in the Playday study, 73 percent said that school is their main opportunity to spend time playing with friends.

Currently, enormous efforts and sums of money are being spent preparing young children for their education. Some of this is based on over-eager parenting; some of it is a creation of pop culture. An entire industry of DVD sales and pre-preschools has sprung up to service the perceived need to create an educational base for children's early school years. As educators, we must ask ourselves fundamental questions about preparing young children for lifelong learning: What skills do they need? What teaching methods and learning theories best address how to build these foundational skills? How do we address the diversity of learners in and bring needed cultural awareness to our classrooms? How do we value the home literacy experiences that children bring to the classroom door?

Giving Value to Preschool Play

Children bring many different learning experiences to the classroom, but some have more than others. Those who have been exposed to daycare or preschool will have already begun to build skills, to engage in "learning how to learn." For children without this type of foundation, reconciling their previous experiences to those of the classroom is more difficult.

Explaining this difficulty becomes easier if we think about how children learn. Learning is a social phenomenon that takes place within a child's cultural world (Street, 2000). Children learn in many ways, active participation in play, planned activities, their own observations, and discussions with adults among them. Social interactions and explorations of their understanding of their world are vital — these are achieved through play (Branscombe, Castle, Dorsey, Surbeck, & Taylor, 2000).

Teachers today have to plan curriculum in key learning areas and build upon children's skills and social interactions to help them learn. My twofold goal in this text is to help teachers understand the importance of play as a pedagogy for learning those early skills and to reach out to learners who are challenged by current classroom practices as well as those children who need to be challenged. This book should be beneficial to educators in Kindergarten to Grade 3 classrooms.

Yet my goal stands in the face of current practice. Schools and teachers have largely abandoned play as a pedagogical tool in favor of the perceived benefits of an academic agenda. At the same time that many parents are beginning to question homework policies, standardized testing, and the lack of socialization skills in children, societal pressures insist that academics become the sole focus in classroom learning. As a result, in many school curricula, play is noted but rarely seen as foundational to young children's literacy building — this is a serious omission.

My intention is to connect children's play to our curricula and pedagogical practices. Teachers understand that children's learning at home scaffolds and connects to school learning — *and much of a child's early life, up to and including the first years in school, is spent playing*. This book goes some distance in offering a look at the benefits of engaging children in a pedagogy that honors what they know and prepares them for later years with a strong literacy foundation. The learning experiences provided by playing at home are of enormous value to what will happen later in the classroom, and this knowledge will enhance the roles of both teachers and parents. Play represents a huge opportunity to create a foundation for the future literacy lives of our children.

Emergent Literacy — Embedded in Social Practices

Emergent literacy, as termed by Marie Clay (1991), is the ongoing and developmental process of understanding and using language from birth until independence. Typically, children from birth to eight years of age are in this phase of development.

Emergent literacy begins with oral language, which is central to how children understand and communicate their needs and wants. Through their experimentation with language — the constructive process of engaging the world around them — and amid its constant feedback, children become competent "meaning makers" (Wells, 1999).

"During early childhood, abilities to represent feelings, intentions, and actions in words, to pretend play, to draw and to construct with blocks emerge. Children begin to build bridges between ideas and to connect feelings, facts, and new understandings. If properly supported in early childhood, children enter Grade 1 eager to learn the cultural tools essential to our society — literacy, numeracy, and inquiry skills."

— Charles E. Pascal, *With Our Best Future in Mind: Implementing Early Learning in Ontario*

According to socio-cultural perspectives, children's home literacy engagements can be viewed as social practices situated within communities (Wenger, 1998). These social practices are ultimately the foundations of children's learning (Roskos & Christie, 2000). Through the early years of play and exploration, children acquire a substantial body of skills and knowledge (Hughes, 1991).

Successful pedagogy recognizes that learning is not confined to the school and can neither begin nor end there. Embracing the valuable learning and language experiences that define children's first literacy engagements with the world is necessary for later success (Heath, 1983).

Children also participate in literacy engagements long before they can discriminate between letters or recognize the correspondences between letters and sounds (e.g., Clay, 1991). From their earliest moments, all children are active learners who construct knowledge and understandings within a series of age-related stages (Piaget, 1962).

The Skills versus Play Debate

Early childhood education is a challenging area that has prompted an ongoing debate about the value of play in early literacy, as opposed to a skills model approach. The skills model is now dominant in North American educational strategies.

The U.S. educational strategy known as "Head Start" places huge value on early childhood skills acquisition. It promotes the social and cognitive growth of disadvantaged children through providing programs in education, nutrition, social needs, and health services to children and families enrolled in the program. Programs such as ABC Head Start Alberta are similar.

In its *National Strategy for Early Literacy*, the Canadian Language and Literacy Research Network (2009) put a focus on skills too, but stated its awareness of stakeholders' expanding definitions of literacy. The Network's report says that "literacy included not only reading and writing, but also speaking, viewing and representing, as well as what these mean to various social and cultural groups." Although this definition acknowledges literacy as a social and cultural practice, Canadian definitions of literacy are still skills based as defined by the International Adult Literacy and Skills Survey and the Adult Literacy and Life Skills Survey; these surveys, conducted by the Organisation for Economic Cooperation and Development (OECD) and Statistics Canada, are quoted in the Network's *National Strategy for Early Literacy* (see p. 11).

One key recommendation of the Canadian Language and Literacy Research Network's report is as follows: "Children acquire fundamental literacy skills through an evidence-based instructional program that must include systematic, direct and explicit instruction, supporting the acquisition of essential alphabetic, code-breaking skills and development of strong oral language, vocabulary, grammar, fluency and comprehension skills" (p. 40).

This recommendation negates children's natural literacy acquisition in their own worlds and on their own terms. In fact, it holds children and play hostage in favor of a political and economic agenda. It ignores theoretical research on children's early literacy skills learning: children achieve language and literacy skills at higher levels when they experience rudimentary play scenarios and creativity in nurturing environments.

A lack of skills for higher order thinking points to the value of play. Despite a heavy emphasis on the 3 Rs in the Kindergarten to Grade 3 curriculum, educators and parents alike see that children often lack such thinking skills as how to make choices, generate solutions, and take risks.

Generally, developing appropriate literacy instruction for the early years is a serious challenge. The programming is specialized and falls largely outside primary and elementary teacher preparation. Although we know and understand that most children pass through stages of physical and intellectual growth, we also know that they do not reach each stage at the same time and that growth is highly individual (Piaget 1962; Clay 1991). Early identification of learning and other developmental difficulties is a challenge, but if met, can lead to interventions, providing more optimal pathways for successful first literacy experiences.

With a full academic agenda, it is difficult for teachers to fit play into the curriculum; however, more research is advocating play as an effective pedagogical tool that centres learning in a holistic environment similar to a home environment. Including play as a pedagogical tool is especially a struggle when teachers lack the specialized skills. By using a natural form such as play, however, we can cultivate children's natural love for learning.

A significant issue for children's early years' curricula is to build a base of knowledge that privileges the social and cultural contexts in which children learn, while focusing on the skills that schools think that children need to be taught.

Issues that affect children's prospects as learners

High child poverty rates are still a huge concern, as child poverty studies suggest that family economics may lead to later inequity in life. Children from poorer families often suffer disproportionately health issues, missed opportunities, underemployment, and social exclusion, all of which can be traced to a lack of early childhood intervention in education.

Research shows how early intervention using activities that engage children and challenge their young minds may affect some of their life path trajectories (Mustard, 2006). Other studies show that one-quarter of Grade 1 students are at risk because of fewer resources in the home. Meanwhile, as a "Survey of Canadian Attitudes toward Learning" found, many Canadians think that early childhood learning should focus more on attitudes, such as fostering a positive attitude towards learning, than on school readiness (Canadian Council on Learning, 2007). All of these considerations need to be part of a teacher education process, if it is to fully engage with the issues facing children preparing for school.

Challenges Facing Play as Learning

The role of play for children has come under much scrutiny by parents and educators. The word "play" once conjured up visions of children engaged in spontaneous thought, movement, and expression. Historically, the word evoked images of carefree children running in fields, playing games, and climbing trees. Now it has acquired another connotation: that of time wasted and educational opportunities lost.

Reasons related to work help explain why play has been relegated to spaces outside of curriculum. In a crowded world, playtime — or to use a favorite term

---

"Play *is* learning for children. Play can be experimentation or an approximation of something the child has experienced in the adult world. Play can both stimulate and be a product of the imagination. Play is the heart of childhood. It is the embodiment of learning, and it provides a time and space where children can be in control of their own lives and their own environments."

— Dr. Joyce Bainbridge

"It is so important to get it right from the start of life and through the school years. Children are remarkably similar at birth, but by age four the gaps are already dramatic. We risk undermining the benefits of our investments in full day learning if we do not address the needs of our very youngest of learners and their parents. And if we do not build on the gains made by the 4 to 5 age group when children enter the primary grade of school those gains will probably be diminished."

— Charles E. Pascal, *With Our Best Future in Mind: Implementing Early Learning in Ontario*

of parents, "quality time" — is often something left when the "real" work has been done. This dichotomy between work and play is formalized in the workplace. Play is not considered to be a productive measure or preparation for the world of work. Unfortunately, this sort of office and organizational thinking is too frequently transferred to the home and classroom.

Many early-grade teachers, who often struggle under the weight of school and societal expectations, worry that they ought to keep schoolchildren almost always engaged in serious learning tasks: tasks that in some obvious fashion prepare them for gainful achievement. This rarely stated (but commonly held) perspective holds that outside the playground, play has no real place in our schools. On one hand, however, schools put great importance on play as a socialization activity; on another, they confine it to physical education classes, lunch break, and recess.

For too long, many educators and parents have undervalued play and viewed it only as a playground or physical education class activity.

Furthermore, although much research shows intricate connections between play and skills development, it is difficult for parents and educators to see how learning gained through play is transferable to work-related skills. Some types of play do not realistically fit within the confines of the structured and expected behaviors of children in the curriculum.

Play as a form of learning is subject to other challenges. The outcomes of play are difficult to quantify. Educators also tend to have set ideas about good and bad play. Meanwhile, the media have pushed the boundaries of childhood outwards, in order to mimic the real-life experiences of adults.

Yet a playful curriculum has much value. Creative in form and innovative in ideas, it produces children who show resilience in the face of change and can share divergent thinking about the everyday nuances that define their lives. The ability to explore and confront such changes prepares children for later experiences where changing patterns in life are becoming more of the norm. *Crisis in the Kindergarten: Why Children Need to Play in School* is a 2009 report from the Alliance for Childhood by directors Edward Miller and Joan Almon. The U.S. report makes this argument: "Creative play that children can control is central to their physical, emotional, and cognitive growth. It contributes to their language development, social skills, and problem solving capacities, and lays an essential foundation for later academic learning" (p. 63).

The literature on play remains supportive of the literacy development of the child. Several researchers (see Dyson, 2003; Edminston, 2007; Gregory, Long, & Volk, 2005; Hall, 2000; and Morrow & Rand, 1991) report that literacy engagements for children are enriched through pretend play. Jane Hewes (2007) says, "In play children explore and test the edges of what they know, where they begin to understand what it feels like to reach for something new, and to achieve something originally impossible, even unimaginable" (p. 33). Seeing the rightful placement of play as a pedagogy that responds to and addresses early literacy and numeracy skills is a return to the natural way in which young children learn.

Play as It Relates to Curriculum Planning

If we agree that play is fundamental to the development and educational success of our students, then the challenge becomes how to bring play into a formalized curriculum, where skills are seen as the focus for future achievement. The following are all aspects of play that need to be considered in its relationship to (and with) curriculum planning for the early grades.

- Children learn in a holistic environment, one that encourages learning through speaking, listening, creative thinking, and moving, all of which are conducive to play-based exercises.
- Learning should be a hands-on experience, with classroom centres that develop independent thinking, learning, and other initiatives driven by children's own desires to learn.
- Children need to learn in spaces that acknowledge and build on the socio-cultural dimensions of home and family that they bring with them to school.
- Since children learn and grow at different rates, we must develop programs that are responsive to every child's needs and that exemplify learning through play as a pedagogy that provides equity. Most effective teachers know they have to be mindful of their students' needs.
- Effective teaching practice means having a philosophy that places play as important to learning and understanding.

Preparing to facilitate play

Play can find a space in classrooms where the teacher has mastered such skills as keenly observing learning moments, sharing and communicating to find children's voices, and using play to help children connect their feelings and thoughts with words. Teaching children how to freely communicate their thoughts and feelings to others is needed if they are to ultimately interact with their world of learning.

In order to successfully introduce or encourage play in their classrooms, teachers need to do the following:

- to model attitudes that recognize and use play in the curriculum as a learning pedagogy
- to gain an understanding of the importance of play and its vital relationship to learning
- to understand how to include appropriate play experiences for young children
- to learn how to contribute to play without controlling children's exploration
- to understand how to encourage particular learning goals in play when working alongside children
- to learn the importance of socio-dramatic play in the construction of children's identities
- to learn to recognize and categorize play for learning

Play as Children's Work and Other Viewpoints

At its simplest, play is children's work and the way in which children inform their formative world (Piaget, 1962). Children's play is used for different functions, such as social engagement, symbolic expression, and motor activity. All of these forms of play show traces of the identities of children and may be an expression of power within themselves and how they communicate with others. Essentially, play is what children do in their world and it is fun. Through it, we see the development of children's cognitive skills, such as fine and gross motor skills; an orientation to their environment; and skills of socialization to play out with others. In many ways, play is the foundation upon which these types of skills for life are built.

The building blocks for life that are found in play-based activities show the intricate link between play and life. Child play gives opportunities to engage children through a performance of life, one that can be experienced in a safe environment. Language and communication skills, problem solving, and the use of critical thinking strategies are all needed. Play is a chance to practise these skills that inform so many aspects of a child's life (Bruner, 1978).

Lenses through which to examine play

The concept of play is both complex and dynamic. Widely differing viewpoints have emerged about young children and play. Young children's language and development is not a fixed field, and the varying issues surrounding play are constantly being re-examined though different lenses.

Play has been studied only in quite recent times. Before the 20th century, most children who did not come from wealthy families spent their time either in an educational system or in work to help support their families. Whatever else they did was of little interest to the adult world. At the turn of the century, the lives of children began to be examined in earnest, in hopes of turning children into better adults.

Psychoanalytical perspectives on play were initially based on the work of Sigmund Freud and then later looked at and revised by others. In Freud's view, child's play offered glimpses into the internal and external development of the id and the ego, with various sexual stages demonstrated along the way. Erik Erickson (1963) believed that children's engagement with play developed their self-esteem, thereby giving children mastery over their thoughts. He reached these conclusions by studying children's body movements, the representational

"It [play] helps you concentrate in school."

"We need fresh oxygen from the playground."
— Children quoted in the 2009 British Playday study

forms children used to communicate their thoughts. Erickson came to realize that children naturally interconnect what they wish to communicate with their activities and social play. In short, children explore challenging play scenarios as a way to respond to the world.

The confidence gained in finding power over a situation that in the real world may be too difficult to confront is empowering to children. Role-playing a teacher or a parent who has authority gives the child a chance to work out different viewpoints, new ideas, or even fantasies of being someone else. Children's play is complex because it mirrors the fantasy as well as the reality of some children's lives. It is played out through an experiential process that sometimes is encouraging to self but also confronts the anxiety and helplessness that may characterize children's lives.

From the work of Lev Vygotsky, a Russian psychologist, we have learned that children individually create knowledge about the world through the interactivity that surrounds, characterizes, and defines their world when they play. Most of us can remember instances where this principle came into being. For example, I visited with a Kindergarten class, where some of the children were playmaking around the fable of the tortoise and the hare. When someone asked where the race could take place, one child immediately suggested the street where the local Santa Clause parade is held, a popular event among the community's children. Another countered with his own residential cul-de-sac, while a third recommended a market area in Bombay often mentioned by older family members. When playing, the children were incorporating their implicit cultural values.

From a socio-cultural perspective, play as experienced as a social interaction is the first and most important encounter with how knowledge informs a child's world. It is how children share their cultural values and beliefs, which are embedded in the scenarios they create. Spontaneous play activities found in childhood show the greatest competencies of children. Exploration of their worlds through the freedom of play leads to new ideas and behaviors to be tried out. These play-based performances show how children develop their own understandings of how to reach out to embrace new skills.

The difference between what a child can do alone as opposed to being in an environment with a supportive individual is called the "zone of proximal development." New skills and development are shown on the part of the child in the presence of another who works to "scaffold" the child's efforts in learning. After acquiring this expertise, the child makes the performance of such skills a part of his or her regular repertoire.

Psychologist Jean Piaget studied children's behavior extensively throughout his life. Piaget (1962) felt that children create their knowledge of the world through individual interactions with people, objects, and materials; this, in turn, leads to a sharing of knowledge based on the children's perspectives. Through play, children test new ideas and learn to regulate their behavior. Piaget focused on two important outcomes of play: first, play brings joy and satisfaction; second, learning is produced through the interaction of play. In his cognitive-developmental stance, learning to regulate one's behavior to show new learning and understanding can be constructed through the many forms of play engaged in by children. Piaget's common-sense views would probably reflect those of many parents and children. His theories about children's development have influenced the entire makeup of grade school curricula.

According to social learning theorist Albert Bandura (1977), children learn social behavior not only through direct experience with an event, but also through observation of what happens and how others act within that event. Any educator will have seen this theory in action, for example, when a child imitates or copies another behavior in anticipation of receiving a reward for that behavior. Teachers often use this behavior as a classroom tool through a compliment/reward system, wherein children learn to follow other children based on the teacher's rewarding of positive efforts.

The Value of Play

Playmaking brings children a greater awareness and understanding of the world in which they live. Sutton-Smith (1971) describes play as an inquiry process that consists of four *ways of knowing*: (1) exploration, (2) testing, (3) imitation, and (4) construction. When children play, they construct an understanding of what the world means for them in their own cultural milieu, using these four ways, together or individually, to create their knowledge base.

By way of illustration, I watched a group of children who devised an imaginary cooking TV show, where recipes were created using symbolic play and representational objects. Through the role play, they shared their understanding of how things are interconnected. For example, they chose brand-name products found in their homes for ingredients in their recipes, discussed the grocery stores where their families shopped, and used cooking vocabulary, such as calling a spoon for serving soup "a ladle."

This exploration of their environment through play shows how children imitate those who are in their lives. Through engagement with their peers, they showed an understanding of the narrative of a cooking show and of the actions of other children in varying contributory roles. When a play narrative is freely explored, we can see how the play of the children changes constantly, illustrating their ways of knowing in areas of exploring, predicting, constructing new meaning, and testing out that meaning with further exploration.

Play enthusiast David Elkind feels that play unifies children's mental, psychological, and socio-emotional development. Elkind argues that in the early years, the function of play is to give children the means for developing a sense of competency, especially a sense of competency of the whole self. When children successfully complete a task or action, they feel good all over — and this is what we want to focus on in building confidence in young children through play. Play has the ability to unify and bring all of these aspects together in the learning development moment.

In summary, play is an important medium to children's social, emotional, and cognitive development (Piaget, 1962). When children play, we see how this holistic engagement invites creative expression — play episodes call for an improvisation of scenarios that show how children must be open to giving and taking ideas during the playmaking. Such playmaking fully involves their imaginations in how they develop symbolic representations of the objects and spaces to satisfy the needs of the play. Children need to be flexible in their thinking and in their ability to explore new options. They have to be able to get across their own ideas to their peers, as well as to understand how they can extend and explore further a given idea.

Play also plays a key role in the development of social confidence. By its collective nature, it requires interaction with others, and the regulation and control over emotions. To take on new roles in play situations, children must share and

"Play takes various forms, but pleasure is at the heart of all play regardless of whether it is word play during creative writing or imaginative play on the schoolyard. Play is motivating and an essential component for learning as it requires children to be active learners and to capitalize on possibilities for the social construction of meaning."
— Dr. Janette Hughes

understand the rules of turn-taking and resolving problems. Interaction and play episodes will naturally bring forth arguments that require children to learn to respect the ideas of others, to cooperate, and to build the foundations of relationships in early friendship. These social skills are much needed in the world of the Kindergarten but also in the world of life.

Physical play has a developmental role, too. It develops large and small motor skills, the idea of safety's role in self-preservation, an understanding of the nutrition needs of our bodies, and trust in our ability to make decisions. Play is vital to all of these processes.

How Children Feel about Playing

The comments given below were all made by children who took part in the 2009 British Playday study. The annual study was coordinated by Play England, an organization that works to ensure that policy makers, parents, and the public recognize the importance of play.

"Play is important because children need to go for a walk and get some fresh air."

"There might as well be no colour if you can't play!"

"It means being able to shout without getting told off!"

"If you learn too much and stuff and it's all in your head, you won't have time to be free and stuff."

"When you play, you can let your imagination unfold."

"Play makes me feel happy."

Come, Play with Me: Types of Play

Sara Smilansky (1968) carried out an important study with preschool children in both the United States and Israel. All of the children came from a lower socioeconomic background. Her observations of children's play are constructed under the following categories: functional play, constructive play, symbolic, or dramatic play, rough and tumble play, and games with rules.

Functional play

Children create, become, and enter imaginary worlds as they choose to find ways to explore varying episodes that mimic real life. Functional play is sometimes known as "practice play." I recall watching my son pretending to start an imaginary car with Mommy's keys, a game of which he never tired. Activities like these can be practised over and over again. You may have heard parents comment about other such repetitive activities, pointing out that their child "does that over and over again." The play, in this case, is a learning opportunity for the child. Focused within such a play scenario, the child pretending to start Mommy's car is refining his motor skills while practising an action that imitates one in the world of adults.

As children learn new skills, even ones as basic as running and jumping, they will perfect these skills through practice. Hopping on one foot around a hopscotch plot shows how they are developing balance, while attempting to do leg splits shows how they build flexibility. Many parents grow tired of the constant "look at me" refrain while their children demonstrate some minor physical achievement; however, the children are demonstrating how practice play leads to self-confidence, success, and control over their bodies and self.

Functional play: *A child named Sarah practises writing her name, gripping the pencil with a fierce concentration as she controls the direction of the "S." Eventually, she fills up the page from the top to the bottom with versions of the letter. This type of writing is not intended for communication, and the writing will not be shared with others. Its purpose is the pleasure of the practice.*

Other types of functional play relate to memory. Listening to children sing the same verse of a song over and over may be dull for the educator, but for the children, it becomes a part of their recall, helping with intellectual sequencing and serialization. An understanding of the meaning entailed in the song, along with ways in which they refine, practise, and succeed with it, develops children's abilities.

Constructive play

Constructive play involves making, building, and creating based on ideas. It is the manipulation of objects, with the goal of creating something new or imagined, as well as putting things together to make representations of reality. Constructive play, such as digging a hole to China and imagining the possibilities of adventure upon arrival, is a form of departure from the world and bridges new understanding. Through engagement of teachers observing and helping them to critically question their assumptions, children may extend their language and conceptual understandings of the world in which they live.

Constructive play — An example of teacher scaffolding: *The teacher produced a large bowl of beads for a Kindergarten class. She demonstrated how to string them onto a piece of twine and then explained how she liked to make a pattern of one red bead, one blue, and one green for a necklace. She cut and knotted some string for the children and then left them to their own devices. Two of the girls produced recognizable necklaces, with the beads in carefully arranged patterns. One boy produced a string with all the beads the same color. Another boy used the beads to create an imitation snake on the table-top. The last boy just played with the beads, filling and emptying the bowl, pretending they were cereal or noodles and he was preparing a meal. Eventually, the teacher spoke to each child, reinforcing the lesson that each had learned through constructive play — patterns, creativity, or imitation.*

Symbolic, or dramatic play

The art of dramatic play happens when children engage in symbolic representation such as using a spoon as a brush. Children may move from role-playing a mother making soup to becoming a hairdresser in a salon. The symbolic representation of various people and literacy events played out show how children's worlds are developed (Bruner, 1990). When the play corresponds to ideas about how to act in our world, it becomes known as "socio-dramatic play." (See Chapter 7 for more information on symbolic play.)

Symbolic play: *Abigail and Teeba have found themselves at a loss that there is no plastic food for them to use in their symbolic play of a picnic in the house corner.*

While busily placing plastic plates and cups in a picnic basket, they discovered that there is no plastic food in the bins because it is being cleaned. They have to use what is on hand to continue to play. . . .

Abigail opens her hand to Teeba, revealing small, plastic-wheel construction pieces she has found in the bottom of one of the bins.

"Look. Let's use these," she says. "They can be our food. See, the shape is like a wheel, like the pasta we have at home."

Abigail picks up a yellow block and says, "This is the cheese."

Rough and tumble play

Combining aspects of both functional play and dramatic play, this form of play accompanies the pretend play. Particular to boys, it is often seen as wrestling or as pretending to be someone else, like a superhero. Playing heroes and victims, children learn to negotiate the roles and choices that they make in real life.

Rough and Tumble Play — Superhero Time

Carol Sanchos, an experienced Grade 1 teacher in a suburban elementary school, is well aware of the attraction little boys have for rough and tumble play, which is often at odds with classroom conventions. During a unit on heroes, she noted how many of the boys were fascinated by superheroes. She decided to build on this using play-based scenarios, to encourage some of the more reluctant writers and classroom participants.

One day she suggested to the class that they each come up with a superhero. They had to pick a name, a power, and a special clothing item the hero had to wear. The only rule was that the superhero's power could not be violent. Many of the children were enthusiastic. Carol did not discourage the discussion that ensued and instead quietly monitored it.

Daniel: My superhero is going to have a mask. He's going to be invisible.

Jeremy: Cool. My guy . . . my guy . . . my guy is gonna look like a rock star.

Daniel: What's his power going to be?

Jeremy: He'll be invisible, too . . . No, he is going to be able to turn to rubber!

Kate: My hero will be named Willow and will be able to turn into a horse . . . see, she has yellow hair and ribbons, just like me.

The project was a huge success, as the children's efforts to draw and create and explore their superheroes' powers through socio-dramatic play spilled over into lunch and play times. Later, the class constructed a series of simple comic-book frames, based on the adventures of a hero they created together.

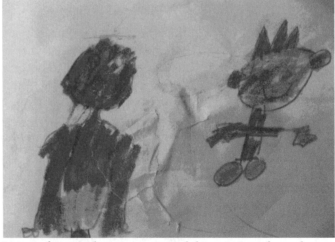

A story of over 12 lines accompanied this painting of superheroes.

Games with rules

Playing with rules means that the child has to acknowledge and accept the rules and conform to the structure of the play. The play is therefore controlled by others. Children struggle with these types of games, as their natural desire is to come up with their own rules. Playing by the rules and conforming to the expectations of a game can be difficult for young children. You may hear cries of "That's not fair," "It's not your turn," and "You're cheating."

Nonetheless, since children desire to be part of the social world, they will want to play rule-bound games, such as computer games, board games, and sports. This type of game playing encourages negotiation and team building.

Playing by the rules: *Geoffrey calls out: "Miss Quinton, Giles is not following the rules of the game!"*

In turn, Giles argues that Geoffrey does not understand the rules of the game.

The teacher, Lisa, then suggests that, as a group, the children define the rules. She tells them that they should try to reach a consensus on the rules and play. Helping to sort out how to play a game and to enjoy the challenges that it may offer is part of the learning gained through rule-bound games — as in this instance, children come to see how rules can create consensus and order in how we do things.

Digging to China: Play as Process

A few minutes spent observing a room full of active children easily confirms the principle that children's play worlds show signs of their active engagement and learning. There is almost always a buzz of energy in the room, as children move from place to place, group to group, and activity to activity. While all that activity may appear chaotic to the onlooker, it is full of new understanding and learning on the part of the players. Knowledge use and exploration of the play world is not static; it is constantly moving and changing as children transform their knowing into something relevant and new. Children are learning all the time, turning every experience into new understanding and new ways of thinking.

Rubin, Fein, and Vandenberg's (1983) criteria define play in terms of dispositions. Essentially, they define what play is and is not. They describe play as providing opportunities to explore process orientation, and as such, play is personally motivating. Play activities can have non-literal characteristics, play need not be governed by rules from outside, and play can be improvised and changed based on the desires of the players.

Play as process orientation

A group of children scramble onto the playground. . . .

"Let's dig a hole," says George.

"Oh, I know, oh, I know, we can make it go somewhere," says Seth, ". . . like China."

"Where's China?" asks a third child.

"Well, I know . . . I know . . . that if you dig really far down you can get there. Let's use these big rocks for shovels. Let's be secret agents and go to China and . . . ," expands George.

"Yeah . . . we can pretend we are rescuing my little brother," says Seth, getting into the spirit of the imaginary exercise. "My mom always asks my little brother if he is digging to China."

They grab rocks and begin to dig deep into the gravel, digging vigorously, their attempt to reach China both exciting and for the moment entirely plausible to them.

This spontaneous play shows the power of imagination and possibility for learning for children. The value of this play to these small friends speaks to the possibility of their successful mission.

The dig for China lasts for three recesses, and a teacher observes how the children are progressing. Engaging in conversation with them, she deliberately asks open-ended questions:

"How is the dig going? When do you think you will arrive there? What is the circle here?" (She points to a drawn circle in the gravel.)

The teacher's questions prompt the children to activate their imaginations but also their problem-solving skills. Back in the classroom, the teacher places relevant books about China on the reading table and points out a Chinese flag on the world map.

The children's chat reveals a great repository of knowledge. They talk about the sizes and shapes of rocks, how to hold your digging rock to get in deeper. Together, they shape the narrative frame of their mission. They discuss among themselves how far away China is, how many planes you might need to take to get there, the fact that it is where the Olympics were held, and how it would take a week to get there on a boat.

The teacher observes how play can be complex and varied, as children verbally create the fantasy of the play and as the mission to China eventually becomes intermingled with a discussion of their upcoming field trip. In this symbolic play scenario, the children are motivated to accomplish this mission. Their vivid imaginations, spurred on by spontaneous play, represent both their real and imagined worlds. Children construct a meaningful place out of their environment, changing and building a scenario as new information is shared. This hands-on activity shows how they experience the play through something they can relate to — playing in a sandbox.

By the third day of the digging to China play, the energy for the dig has dwindled, and two of the children have wandered off to test their skills on the bars. One child remains at the dig site, working diligently to find China.

Sharing their previously acquired knowledge gave the boys opportunity to investigate their world using all of their senses, problem-solving together as they built their story narrative. In all facets, these children have learned through active engagement.

The process orientation of the play allows children to create meaning in their imagined worlds. In the above observation, we see how children's attention is really focused on the process of finding an imagined space. The end product has not necessarily consumed the children's interest. Although the original goal was to reach China, several times the three children abandoned that play to create their "garage," a space in the dirt to place their digging rocks, as well as straws and other small toys. They thereby shifted the play to engage in offshoots of the original narrative.

Process orientation is a shifting of understanding or learning through the play itself. What the product may entail is not necessarily important; however, it is important for children to achieve this act of learning and to develop these skills during the play. Children may be focusing on the making of a nameless product, but that does not negate the importance of what they are doing. It is not just copying the rays of the sun from the teacher's illustration onto their own calendar or pasting the body of a snowman together. What is important is watching how scissors cut the paper, how the glue can stick things together, or beginning to understand how to represent the physical world through art. This process orientation in play is important to children's development and key to their orientation to their world. While adults may misunderstand the process because it seems to shows a lack of focus, children's easy tendency to become distracted is part and parcel of a process orientation. It is how they come to understand how things work.

Intrinsic motivation

In the digging to China play scenario, all three children were intrinsically motivated to achieve their goal, which had little to do with basic needs or the demands of their peers. Their enthusiasm shows how they worked together in the process of the playmaking. Each day the children stepped outside the classroom door and were motivated by the play.

The defining of the play in the dig to China shows many opportunities for the children's learning, as well as demonstrating how the children are intrinsically motivated to play. Motivation to play can arise from a number of sources. For example, the creation of imagined worlds may derive from a child's particular desire to be in an individual space. Left alone, children will initiate spontaneous and motivated play scenarios that bring them great joy and satisfaction, and allow them to show power over their own learning and play.

Teachers need to keep in mind the importance of self-initiated play and motivated play activities. Children derive great enjoyment and satisfaction from them, despite their being void of adult input. The process of digging to China was inherently rewarding for the three children. No concrete lesson was achieved, but as pointed out above, how they are learning to orient themselves within the world is important. Although the intrinsic aspects of the play were not obvious, this does not make them less valuable to the children's learning.

Non-literal play

Non-literal, or free, play calls for free thinking and exploration. As children engage in the narrative frames of play, they engage new possibilities and extensions for their play. New environments and problems are developed and subsequently played out as they explore the "what if," the endless possibilities that free play opens up. Children are often willing to suspend the world of reality, using everyday objects to suit whatever their narrative play frame requires. For the young diggers, straws became shovels and small erasers, dump trucks.

The dialogic engagement between children in play can encompass both their real and imaginative worlds. A teacher watching this type of play can often see how a child's home reality is represented. This type of play may demonstrate what they know, what they don't know, what they are trying to bring to the learning experience, and what they are trying to negotiate. The non-literal quality of play shows the child's ability to negotiate new experiences, a needed skill for life.

Experimentation with rules

Another characteristic found in play is children's enormous desire to experiment with rules. Play is improvised and constantly alters the rules about what can and cannot happen. Children's play is in a constant state of negotiation. The rules of play, and by transference the rules of social negotiation, are greatly dependent upon the prior knowledge and the cultural background that children bring to the play space. These rules are implicit and often cannot be articulated to adults. Young children do not like to be bound by rules and come to accept rules and governing instructions only over time. In many of their other interactions, say, with parents or caregivers, they have no control over rules and must accept them at face value. Experimentation with the play rules provides a safe opportunity for problem solving, critical thinking, and risk taking.

During the dig to China, the children negotiated where to dig "to make a difference" and where to locate the garage for the tools. They changed the rules of the game to suit whatever the interest of the moment was. Children's experimentation with rules allows them to gain problem-solving abilities and perhaps to see into the worlds of others. During play like the dig, children easily develop mutual understandings of the forms for the play. The flexibility of their own rules teaches them a host of useful knowledge, not the least of which is how to negotiate with the world around them.

Mental engagement

Play is hard work. The mind is engaged with the construction and reconstruction of the world. Inquiry-based learning requires focus and concentrated engagement. It is in a constant state of design and redesign, in order to accommodate the suggestions of the play scenario.

As noted earlier, in a very real way, play is the work of a child. Furthermore, it is not just a way to engage children until they are ready to take on more tacit and intellectual feats, as is often interpreted in books that encourage early language development in babies. Work by David Elkind (1981), as well as many others, warns that the substitution of play for instructional methodology produces what he calls "the hurried child," the child who is an anxious and dependent follower rather than a self-confident person. As we shall see, play can be a valid and useful part of the classroom experience, one that produces learning as valuable to a child's self-expression, self-worth, and self-enhancement as more conventional learning methods.

"The human need to play is a powerful one. When we ignore it, we feel there is something missing in our lives."
— Leo Buscaglia

2

Learning to Communicate through Play

When children are playing happily, they are also developing a sense of well-being. These feelings of comfort and security help them to regulate their emotions and give them opportunities to develop their interpersonal skills. In turn, these are able to help children become better communicators — and good communication is the foundation of effective speaking and listening.

Inviting children to explore language in playful ways will help them to think creatively. In doing so, the process by which they engage in language for problem solving and use language for varying forms of communication will become more enriched. For children to become masters of their language, they need many opportunities to test these skills, processing their creative energy through repetitive attempts.

Building a classroom environment where children can seek out different challenges and risks in order to become better communicators will provide skills essential for literacy in the 21st century. Not all children begin their learning in language-enriched environments, so critically learning how language sounds, how words are used in communication, and what they mean is central to a balanced language arts program.

Children need to be engaged and interacting with language all the time for the proper development of these skills. Watching children at play shows how they can use language for their own good.

Piaget's cognitive developmental stance talks about active engagement through play, as children practise what they know and risk new experiences through testing and trying things out. As an example, my five-year-old nephew Steven loves to play Restaurant; he brings the menus, checks our fridge to see if he has the ingredients, and pretends to write a list of what we order, discussing all the while which dishes he feels are healthiest for us. After enacting this restaurant scenario many times, Steven asked his parents if he could go to a "real restaurant with table cloths." Bravely, his parents decided it was a good time to let him have this experience. As soon as they had ordered their food, Steven advised the waiter that he had to check the fridge to make sure that the restaurant had the ingredients to make his meal.

Vygotsky reminds us that children's play worlds help develop their thought processes. During recess one day, one of my students asked me to hold his "plane ticket" (a field trip permission slip with a suitable airline symbol pasted on the folded paper). He announced that he was going to Florida for the winter break and would be leaving with many of his classmates at playtime after lunch. As I listened, I could hear familiar airport codes and an announcer saying, "Plane 424 leaving now for Florida — bring your ticket." Children arrived with their own versions of tickets. (Children often will use objects and represent these things as others.) Sounds of "Please buckle up" and "Passport here" were heard. Playing airport for these children was an inroad to discussions about travel, holidays, and family times, but more important, it made a contribution to their language development: they were able to gain practical understanding of the vocabulary of travel and location.

Oral Language Development as Part of Emergent Literacy

Often overlooked in the race to teach young children to read is the development of their oral language abilities. Many children struggle with oral language, and strategies that involve play often prove helpful.

By way of definition, when we speak of *oral language*, we are referring to abilities that involve children's skills at speaking and listening. More specifically, we are referring to children's ability to acquire vocabulary and language, their phonological awareness, their knowledge of letters and words, comprehension of meaning, as well as their ability to follow storytelling, read-alouds, and other narratives.

When children come to school, and during their first years, they are still very much in emergent literacy, busy constructing their understanding of language, how it works, and how it is relevant to their needs and lives. Over time, they understand that language and its use is critical to their being able to engage with others socially. They learn that language serves a purpose and is used in differing contexts, and that understanding these differing contexts will be beneficial to them.

Researchers William Teale and Elizabeth Sulzby (1986) studied children's emergent literacy for some time and reached a number of conclusions about how it works. Their ideas serve as simple guidelines for us as educators, when we begin to assist children in attaining oral language development.

1. Literacy develops when children interact with reading, writing, and oral language in their homes and communities. That is where they learn what language is, how to use it, and what purposes it can serve.
2. Children's literacies begin to emerge long before they enter school. Within their families and communities, they have acquired many skills.
3. These home- and family-based experiences contribute to later formal literacy education and are crucial to their overall language development.
4. Interactions with adults are crucial in laying the foundations for children's language and literacy development.
5. All children learn and acquire language at different rates and move through stages at different speeds.

Although "school literacy" has often been rather narrowly perceived as only reading and writing, early learning for young children is multimodal; in other words, children use many differing text forms to engage in literacy acts (Kress,

2005). These include speaking, gesturing, aural communication, and other forms of personal expression, such as drawing.

The process by which children use these language forms is developmental. It begins at birth, continues throughout childhood, and carries on into adulthood. The playmaking in the early years of children's lives, however, plays a formal role in their ability to communicate. Children experience literacy within environmental and social contexts that help them make sense of how their reading and writing fit within their own social world and the one around them. As emerging readers and writers, children want to make sense of what they read and write. They benefit when they can use these skills in meaningful activities that require active participation. An example is outlined below.

Laura, who had just begun teaching in a Grade 1 classroom in St. John, New Brunswick, was making great efforts to locate the children's reading and writing within their local community. To encourage children to build their oral skills, she began a discussion about the farmers' market that had opened. She brought in newspaper clippings, discussing the idea of a market, and asked the children to help make a list of the jobs at the market. Children engaged in small-group discussions about the jobs, having such conversations as the following.

Henry: When my grand-dad took me to the market last week . . . I mean Saturday . . . um . . . we bought hot chocolate and waffles. . . . I know that could be a job. Someone sells hot chocolate and waffles.

Madison: Yeah . . . Yeah . . . I got hot chocolate, too. You know what . . . you know what? I think that when we went, we got eggs. Yeah, we did.

George: You know what you were saying (gesturing to Madison), we could have someone to take the . . . take the money. Yeah, that would be good.

This discussion encouraged the children to use their oral and communication skills to share what they already knew about jobs at the market. Laura drew on their discussions, asking for each group to share one idea. The discussion included all the children and provided a mutual understanding of the local market. Laura bridged this knowledge to a writing and representation activity.

Children made multimodal representations of what they knew to share with others. They worked in small groups, drawing pictures in comic-strip form of what each person would do at a market. The children thereby shared their literacy experiences in a way that evolved from their social and environmental contexts.

Laura also used their understanding of what it meant to communicate within a group. Some children drew a road map of how to get to the market, showing various familiar store and restaurant signs, such as McDonald's, and a nearby fire station. Another group drew and cut out pictures of vegetables that would be sold, and discussed colors of vegetables and tastes according to color. One boy reported he felt that green vegetables should not be eaten, while another child argued strongly about the virtues of a balanced diet. Later on, one group of the children decided to use puppet role-playing about shopping at the market, furthering their oral skills in playmaking.

Students in one group discussed the colors and tastes of vegetables at the market after drawing pictures of common ones.

This vignette shows us how children engage in many different language processes to inform themselves of the world around them. The processes of oral language call upon all the social and cognitive ways in which children come to literacy. Meaning is gained from active participation, where children construct social understanding — in this case, of the market — as well as from their skills and knowledge, shared in their oral language and play-based activities. Based on this vignette, we can confirm the importance of the knowledge that children bring to the classroom.

Literacy is socially constructed, and in this example, we see how the children develop this in the context of the farmers' market. They interact with one another, adopting differing forms, such as speaking and listening, problem solving through discussion, writing, role-playing, and drawing, and we gain insight into the rich literacy context that forms the basis of children's knowledge. These children share what is called their "funds of knowledge," which Moll, Amanti, Neff, & Gonzales (1992) defined as the ways in which we all form understanding of our experiences.

Oral language must be seen as a part of everyday living that is socially and culturally situated (Barton & Hamilton, 2000). Embracing the valuable learning and oral language experiences that define children's first literacy engagements with the world is needed for later success (Heath, 1983). Teachers who see the value of embedding oral language in how children view the world and within their individual contexts ultimately empower the foundations of literacy that children have when they come to school.

Sounds and Letters — Making the Links

Most children can speak quite clearly long before they can read. Many will have some grasp of the links between sounds and letters, via constant recitation of the ABCs. Discovering that letters can have more than one sound or be combined to create more sounds can be difficult to grasp. Although that is just one part of the puzzle, it is also one necessary to successful reading and writing.

As stated earlier, the best way to ensure that a child successfully navigates the shoals of emergent literacy is through the provision of a stimulating home life and community, full of play and opportunities for language use. Consider, though, that most parents will have only a vague recollection of the term *phonics*, one area in which their children will need help. As we know, phonics essentially describes the relationship between the sounds of language and the written letters, or combinations of letters. These sounds are called "phonemes."

When introducing phonics concepts, adults will find it valuable to remember that children need to hear language in a familiar and meaningful context. Emphasizing the sounds of words as opposed to just saying the words and the letters will greatly help children in their efforts to become readers. Be sure to remind parents that this should be a logical extension of their current playful conversation and coaching, rather than any obvious effort.

Exploring phonemes

Phonemes, the sounds that make up the auditory form of the English language, are represented by letters and groups of letters. While many phonemes use just one letter, some use two or three. In most standard North American English dialects, there are about 40 sounds but only 26 letters to represent them. Various combinations of letters are required to create the rest of the sounds, /ch/ and /th/ being two obvious examples. Some groups of different letters can be used to make the same sound, too. For example, the hard /a/ of "bake" and the /a/ sound in "gain" are made by different letters. Spelling is not necessarily a good guide for phonemes; for example, the hard /e/ sound can be made several ways (e.g., **feet** and **bea**t).

While there are six vowels — a, e, i, o, u, and y — there are 10 distinct vowel sounds used in English, not all of which correspond to their originating vowel. These include the short /e/ (beg), long /e/ (beet), short /a/ (bat), long /a/ (fate), short /o/ (blog), long /o/ (blow), short /i/ (fit), long /i/ (fight, my), short /u/ (luck), long /u/ (duke), and other vowel-based sounds, like /oi/ (toy), /oo/ (fool), and /ear/ (gear). Keep in mind that if a child has been exposed to other languages, he or she may have knowledge of even more sounds. French and Spanish, for example, are quite common in North America, and both contain vowel sounds that differ widely from those used in English.

Consonant phonemes are a bit easier, often corresponding more specifically to the alphabet sounds a child may already know. Phonemes made from combined letters — such as *ch* (chair), *sh* (shop), and *th* (this) — will take longer to get established.

On the next page is a line master that can be shared with the parents of the students in your class.

Phonics in the Home — Helping Your Child

Here are some playful ways to engage your child in exploring sounds and letters.

- Bring words and sounds into your conversation. For example, if you see a train, talk about the sounds it makes: "The train goes choo-choo; you need to put a *c* and an *h* together to make that sound."

- Occasionally, read aloud books that use a lot of alliteration, such as Janet and Allan Ahlberg's *Each Peach Pear Plum* or Jeffie Ross Gordon's *Six Sleepy Sheep*. Encourage your child to speak the words with you after a few readings. Once you feel your child is ready, ask him or her to sound out words based on the first letter.

- Read alphabet books, or make one together by drawing fancy letters or cutting out letters from print advertisements and catalogues.

- Make up flashcards that show simple sound units, such as short /u/ or /b/ — these are called "phonemes." Ask your child to say them aloud.

- Point out letters, and their sounds, in your environment: "Look. That sign says 'STOP.' Can you make that sound?"

- Play letter-based scavenger and treasure hunts: "Can anyone find a word in the playroom that has the /oo/ sound?"

- Place plastic magnetic letters on the fridge and play this game perhaps during meal preparation times: "Can you find the letters to make a /b/ sound? a /th/ sound?" Alphabet blocks can serve the same function.

- Share tongue twisters with children. The tongue twisters help them appreciate the differences between sounds, while still providing amusement. The old favorite "She sells seashells at the seashore" is a great example, but there are many others.

Tongue twisters

A big bug bit the little beetle, but the little beetle bit the big bug back.
Double bubble gum, bubbles double.
Betty bought butter but the butter was bitter, so Betty bought better butter to make the bitter butter better.
A sailor went to sea / to see what he could see. / And all that he could see / was sea, sea, sea.
How much wood could a woodchuck chuck if a woodchuck could chuck wood?
I scream. You scream. We all scream for ice cream!

Early Understandings about Talk

At an early age children develop their understanding of how language works. Parents are amazed at how quickly children discover that language serves differing purposes depending on the ways and context of use. Children learn through language — what and how it is used — to communicate with others. Early language use sees children developing a wide range of vocabulary and expressions depending on whom they are speaking to.

Young children develop many understandings about talk. For example, they understand how we use our voices according to the context — quiet voices for the classroom and outside voices for the playground. Children also quickly understand that language and its appropriate use are balanced according to the circumstances. Children's ability to appreciate that language is afforded particular spaces shows their understanding that all language serves a purpose. Therefore, we must ensure that talk is purposeful and planned so that young children learn the appropriate places and contexts for its use.

To become good communicators, children need particular skills that can be both taught and practised. Taking turns when sharing ideas, negotiating differences in opinions, and learning how to share information individually as well as in a group are important beginning steps for children. Giving children the opportunity to both talk and listen to one another is crucial in early years' settings. Sharing and explaining their thoughts and opinions builds confidence within the children.

Planning for Meaningful Talk

"Talking is important for literacy, for thinking, and for socializing with others. Children should be encouraged to share their experiences, to listen and ask questions. Language development is supported by reading and other forms of expression, including drawing, painting, building and writing."
— Charles E. Pascal, *With Our Best Future in Mind: Implementing Early Learning in Ontario*

Children learn through meaningful engaged interactions whereby they share in the literacy event. When children see the benefit of talking, to share and explore their ideas, they become engaged in developing their own literacy.

Encouraging young children to use language in a purposeful manner is needed not just so they can share ideas in collaborative settings, but also to help them cope with conflicts that are sure to arise in an early years' setting. Inexperienced with conflict, children need opportunities to explore ways to resolve problems through playmaking. Helping children find the appropriate forms of language and the ways in which to express their feelings acceptably prepares them for more formal schooling tasks. Regulation of their emotions happens when children feel that they are competent communicators. Children have a strong sense of injustice and can feel isolated if they have been wronged in some way. Learning to read children's non-verbal expressions, such as their facial expressions, gestures, and posture, helps educators understand the children's needs. The larger numbers of children coming to school with delayed speech abilities also require educators to pay more attention to children's non-verbal communication (Canadian Language and Literacy Research Network, 2009; Miller & Almon, 2009). Understanding the attached meanings that children associate with these forms of communication will help us to communicate with them and to build on their language skills. Although we may not always be aware of our own actions as teachers, we need to be sensitive to the non-verbal messages that children can easily pick up on.

Communicating through Charades

Trevor has a large class of Grade 1 students, with children from many backgrounds and ethnicities. Some of them have poor oral skills, and a number of them are English language learners. After several attempts to draw out some of the more reluctant communicators, he stumbled across a good classroom game, the old favorite Charades. He simplified the game and the rules, so that one child acted out a household task, while three other children with varying skills tried to guess what the student was doing.

"I asked them to explain what the actor was doing," said Trevor. "The key thing was that the children were so focused on what the actor was doing, they didn't worry about how they were saying it. The game also really appealed to their sense of humor — they loved to play it, even the students with little English."

Helping Children Communicate

- Model good listening for the children. Hold eye contact as they talk to you. For children who are more physically active, hold a hand to show that you are still listening, even if they find it difficult to keep eye contact.
- Observe and respectfully acknowledge the importance of the messages that children communicate to you. Ask yourself questions like these: "Do I understand the message?" "What did the child want me to say?" "Is there something else they wanted to share?"
- If children find it hard to talk, lend them your voice. Guide their conversations through bridging. Model how we talk and what we are learning. "Did you mean this, Meena?" (Repeat and offer more explanation.) "Tell me again."
- Use positive language to reinforce ideal behavior with others. "You are a good friend, Jenna, to help Henry with the blocks. I liked how you explained what we were doing. It is so important that we understand one another."

We want children to actively engage in authentic talk in creative ways that encourage them to use their imaginations. To become active participants in the classroom's circle of conversation, children need to see the use of questioning. Creating a classroom that invites creative thinking in the form of questions will inspire listening and speaking. Educators must hypothesize, imagine, wonder, project, and otherwise see the possibilities for positive conversation around them. Doing this builds a classroom with meaningful talk.

To place this idea in a classroom setting, remember that almost all children are inspired and curious about topics that grab their interest. They like to find out more about these topics. Children also intuitively understand that particular subjects locate them in social and cultural contexts, and these identities are closely linked to the talk children choose to pursue.

For example, my own son likes to chat about video games, the various arcade games, and in particular, how to get to the coveted "next level" in a game. Both he and his friends associate video games with being mature and skilled. He likes to show me how he is gaining in play and what new levels he has achieved. Showing a sincere interest in what my son likes to discuss, and following his lead, has helped in his language acquisition.

Developing Speech Confidence

- Confidence is built through a safe and secure classroom, where children feel their opinions are valued.
- Draw out children's discussion by adding to what they have said. For example, if Gemma shows you her new rubber boots, share and build a discussion. "I like your new boots. They are red and blue. Wow! Look at the red stripes on the side! Do you like walking through puddles?" Let children hear you use descriptive language in a context that they understand. Remember, children naturally absorb language and make it their own.
- Make an effort to connect to a child's experiences and extend the conversation. If John tells you that he is going to visit his grandmother, ask him what he will do at his grandmother's home. Keeping the conversation going lets the children know you are interested in them. It teaches children that communication requires attention and concentration — it is a two-way process.
- Offer access to games and activities that give many opportunities for chat, listening, and discussion.
- Provide an environment that celebrates all cultural groups and that encourages language representation from the entire group.

Drawing on the senses

Children always learn better when there is a sensory component to the play and learning scenario. With the basic games outlined below, a teacher can utilize their natural sensory curiosity to enhance their speech and oral expressiveness.

- Children love to collect things from nature. Go on a nature walk and collect stones, leaves, shells, bird's feathers, tree bark, flowers, berries, and nuts. Ask children to touch these and use sensory language to describe how they feel. Also ask them to describe the shapes of things, their sizes, and whether they can compare them to other familiar objects.
- Ask children to talk about the differences in how things taste, for example, between green and black grapes, or red and green peppers. (You can also discuss how people are the same and different, a healthy thing to do and a way to respect what makes us unique.)

Games That Encourage Talk
- Board games
- Guess Who?
- Memory games
- I Spy
- Hangman
- Jeopardy

Building Classroom Listening Skills

- Show and share promotes speaking and listening. Children can bring objects and talk about them, a good way for English language learners to share their culture. Challenged or shy learners can show a picture or have a puppet to describe their object.
- Use story bags that contain a good-quality storybook with materials that help to support the story. Support materials may include puppets, soft toys, games, or related objects. An informational text that can be related to any part of the narrative may be included. Sometimes, a CD or cassette can be played to help children follow along the story.

- Puppet theatres and puppets allow young children to overcome inhibitions and use their own voices to structure a narrative. The use of puppets encourages dialogue and discussion with shy students.
- Action songs and nursery rhymes help children bring actions and music together; they also help them develop a greater awareness of rhyme.
- Role-play allows for children to try on different roles and personas. These play scenarios need not be fantastical. Children love to play in imaginary spaces that reflect the neighborhoods where they live, such as a pretend post office or grocery store.
- A listening area with pre-recorded stories is helpful to children.
- Having children working in pairs encourages them to verbalize and clarify the thoughts in their heads before group discussion. It also encourages good listening, not to mention social skills.
- You can ask children to organize themselves in a straight line according to a specific criterion, such as shoe size, height, or colors. Encourage them to talk with and listen to one another in order to complete the task.
- Soundscapes provide a good way to have children develop discerning listening skills. Via the Internet, you can easily find soundscapes. Once you share one with the class, ask the students as a group to identify what they heard, and record their findings. Children can also create remembered sounds, such as those of a windstorm or rainstorm, using hand-made instruments.

Sharing their learning

Children love to share what is important to them. Teachers who allow students to share their successes and news in the classroom are actually allowing them to talk about their literacy engagements. When this involves an informal sharing of the learning that has taken place at a literacy centre, it asks the child to account for what has been learned and to set goals. Teachers then have a chance to clarify and extend some of the learning they have observed.

Narrative retelling, where a teacher asks a child to describe in more detail the topic of interest, is also important. It can scaffold greater vocabulary. Ideally, the child will retell a story in his or her own words.

Read-alouds for listening comprehension

Read-aloud is among the most significant experiences children can have in terms of their language and literacy development. It is a way for children to increase their listening comprehension. We know from research that when they listen to literature throughout the day, children uncover new meanings and learn to make insightful connections to their own lives (Galda, Ash, & Cullinan, 2000). With help from the teacher, they can make these connections to the world around them.

Reading aloud is a sharing of language. Hearing the language of stories and informational texts exposes children to written language structures and more complex vocabulary and difficult concepts than they would hear in normal conversation. Making all genres of children's literature a part of the reading experience in a classroom appeals to many different tastes, as can be confirmed while watching the choices children make in their library selections.

The read-aloud itself allows the teacher to encourage oral language. First, give a brief introduction to the book and explain why you chose it. Show the cover illustration and title, and ask the students what they think the book may be about. Respond to any questions that arise as you read or build on students' ideas and understandings. Once in a while, stop and ask for predictions of what will happen next. Be sure to ask open-ended questions. Share what parts you liked and invite the students to do the same.

Read-alouds can be extended in many ways. They permit the teacher to scaffold the children's discussion, thereby encouraging children to make more connections. Dramatic play based on part of the story is an interactive engagement with story. After a read-aloud, the teacher may suggest that children respond at the Writing Centre through writing and drawing (see Chapter 3). Symbolic representation of characters through cutouts enables children to share connections from their own lives.

Storytelling — Understanding the Nature of Story

In Leslie's Senior Kindergarten classroom, a reading of the book *The Paper Bag Princess* by Robert Munsch introduces students to many forms of language. They engage in both reading and a critical sharing of viewpoints; through her questioning, Leslie helps children to understand both the narrative form of story and some relevant themes.

After an animated reading of the book, which is about a girl who defies gender stereotypes to become a princess on her own terms, Leslie engages her class in a discussion of friendship, stereotypes, and gender.

Leslie: What did you like about the story? Kieran?

Kieran: Well, I liked the end. I think that Ronald is a bad friend . . . a bad prince.

Leslie: You do? Why is he not a good friend? Why do you think that?

Kieran: Because even when Elizabeth saved him from the dragon he did not say thank-you. He told her to change her dirty clothes because she did not look like a princess.

Daneisha: (interjecting) . . . yeah, that, and also too that he thinks that she should wear princess clothes.

Leslie: Do you think princesses should always dress a certain way?

Daneisha: They wear pink, I know *(listening to others talking about what princesses should wear)* . . . but, you know, she saved him from the dragon and got her clothes burned for him. He is a bum. *(repeating the last line of the book)*

Leslie: And so he is not a good friend?

Seth: No, not a good friend. He just wants everyone to be the way he wants.

The children express their understanding through play at the classroom centres. At the Writing and Drawing Centre, children re-create the story in a collaborative setting, as they decide what parts of the story need to be illustrated and shared.

These student images were inspired by a reading and discussion of The Paper Bag Princess.

Children also re-create and re-enact the main points of the story using costumes, while others work on building the castle in the block area. Other children repeat parts of the story using the puppets in the dramatic play area. The classroom is alive as the children create and re-create the story narrative, honing their oral language skills.

Stories as identity

Stories are a part of all of us. They are a vital way in which we learn about who we are and the nature of the world around us. Watch storytime at a library sometime — even without the visual excitement of the screen, children can still be seen intently listening and watching, as the story unfolds through the expression in the narrator's voice paired with the illustrations of the picture book.

Oral storytelling requires children to exercise concentration and memory if they are to grasp what the story is about. Well read or told, a good story will capture children's sense of wonder, confirm what they know and understand, and expand upon their interests and curiosity. Listening to stories about other children and other parts of the world will require them to share the viewpoints and emotions of others. Through the shared listening experience, children can also learn to appreciate different opinions and viewpoints, as they are exposed to them.

Inside the narrative structure

In creating a classroom where others and their viewpoints are accepted, we want our choice of literature to provide new learning, but also to help children understand the patterns and sequences by which we make sense of our world. Whether this is through a book about the passage of the seasons or use of a Robert Munsch story to make a moral point, the narrative structure, or an organizational map for this learning, is a necessary element of the early-grade classroom. Through the critical thought process that comes with storytelling and subsequent discussions, children come to understand new vocabulary, and how (and when) it may have different meanings. By an interconnecting of the written text and picture book illustrations, students also come to understand that the two aspects work together to create meaning in the narrative structure. This insight assists them in oral language when they are retelling the story to others.

In Leslie's classroom, children used their expressive language and became part of a critical discussion about how the protagonist stands up for herself — they questioned stereotypical viewpoints on dress and image. Through their play, we note how they developed their oral language and shared their critical understanding of *The Paper Bag Princess*. (See the drawing and sequencing of the story on the previous page.) In Leslie's play-based classroom, other activities, such as puppet play, allowed children to explore what it means to judge people by their clothes. The students decided that Prince Ronald was "just behaving badly." Building upon this response, Leslie asked them to retell the story using the puppets. As they did so through their play, children shared the voices of the characters as well as catch phrases from the picture book — their comprehension was empowered.

Verbal retelling of the story showed the children's understanding of a complex theme, such as identity. Their addition of a scene, one where the prince apologizes to the princess, showed how they explored the varying ideas within the plot and extended original ideas. In this case, the children's small-group discussions led to explorations of the themes. Collaborative play through painting, drawing, puppet acting, and role-play using a blocks area to create the castle setting enabled the children to feel and live the story; it reinforced the narrative structure and allowed them to use their own words and draw on their own cultural understandings. The imaginative play that ensued throughout the day developed the children's oral language, some of which was quite complex. Children shared differing viewpoints of the characters, perspectives, and ways to address acceptance and difference.

Telling and engaging with stories

Storytelling is very much a performance. Creating the environment for children to listen to and experience a story requires teachers to make use of voice and specific mannerisms, and to develop a persona that is both inviting and engaging. Children draw on their imaginations to engage in many play scenarios. Using these forms helps children play out stories for further character exploration and their understanding of narrative forms. The following recommendations offer specific ways in which an educator can then expand upon the themes and ideas of a story, using play scenarios.

- Make use of storyboards; ask children critical questions about the characters to show how the characters could change their situations.
- The use of puppets lets children express the characters' voices and the viewpoints that they may have about the narrative retelling.
- Having children use musical instruments at the appearance of a character or for a scene change helps them to understand the framing and sequencing of story.
- Have children explore how music can create a particular setting for the action in the story. Attaching music to particular contexts and setting can encourage imaginative thought.
- Passing children objects that may be found in the story from a story bag and asking them to continue a retelling of the story with their own voices builds confidence with storytelling and narrative frame understanding.
- Using pictures and photographs contributes to the imaginative creation of the story. By way of example, a teacher could follow up an animal story by holding a picture of a dog and saying, "This is a picture of my dog and he is . . ."

Teachers can also use the stories of children's lives as a way to promote oral communication. In the vignette that follows, a Grade 2 teacher shows how events outside the school may be honored and given a place in developing children's oral skills.

Teacher Kelly Ellis honors the home literacy of her students. She believes that parents hold an important key to their children coming to understand stories. In her Grade 2 class, each student is asked to share a scrapbook of a special family event. Adam, an English language learner, shared his trip to the zoo to see polar bears. When he spoke to the class about his trip, Kelly assisted him through prompting and putting the event in a narrative form.

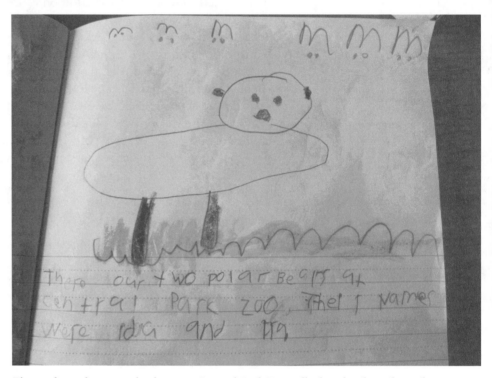

The student who saw polar bears at Central Park Zoo talked to the class about the experience after illustrating and writing about the event.

Creating Space for Listening

Listening skills, which all children need to develop, take practice. For many of the children you teach, storytelling and read-alouds, as well as the listening skills that go with them, will have occurred only at bedtime. Before you begin a story in a classroom, remind them to adopt a "listening formation," such as legs crossed, with hands in laps and eyes focused on you. Keep in mind that for many children who are read to at home, they may be used to listening lying down. This practice is fine, too, if the classroom space allows it. Whether they are sitting or lying, their comfort level will determine how attentive they are.

Space can be an issue. For many of the classrooms I have visited, I have noticed that neither the outdoor physical space nor the classroom space may be there for what you want to do. Some early years' teachers use a quilt or a piece of material to indicate the space where the story will be shared.

Effective teachers draw upon the imaginative abilities of children when engaging them in storytelling. When I spent time observing primary teachers in

London, England, I found that even though their school structure varies from those in North America, they used similar strategies for storytelling. For example, in her early years' classroom in inner-city London, Karen Norman invites children to use their imaginations and to travel by rocket ship to the planet "Imagination." She asks children to imagine themselves in a space where all stories can become real and true. "Now let's pretend that we have just landed on our special place, find a space where you are comfortable — imagine that you are there." Here, the invitation for the story session makes it more intimate for the children. Children are listening and focused. They want to engage in the creative playmaking when the time comes.

Building Story Skills

Story skills can be created and enhanced using any number of educational tools, from wordless picture books to simple finger puppets.

Use wordless picture books to teach children how to read and understand illustrations.

Children marvel at the opportunity to provide the text to accompany the visuals in wordless books. It is a great way for them to develop their oral language and written skills. Wordless books vary in the degree of complexity. Some plots are easier to follow through the illustrations than others. Since all wordless books draw upon the creative imagination of the reader, this type of book appeals to young and older children alike. Wordless books may be shared to show the sequencing of a plot. Children can talk about what they may already know from the illustrations and can be encouraged to share other understandings of the narrative. Guiding the children with "thinking" questions can be helpful: What is happening in this picture? How do you know? What do you think comes next? And why is that? The rich detail offered in wordless books invites children to share other memories or experiences they may have had. Focusing the children's attention on the visual asks for them to develop their observation skills, which are needed for our increasingly visual world.

Use sounds and music as a way to build the story frame.

In building the children's auditory skills, the use of simple sound effects to create the settings for stories and develop the events can be very enjoyable. Being able to recognize particular sounds — for example, a doorbell, the wind, or animals — helps children to identify vocabulary that can be used for building transitions within a story. A story that builds on repetition can reinforce particular vocabulary and transitions within the story. In "The Three Billy Goats Gruff," for instance, you can ask the children what kind of sound the smallest goat would make as he crosses. Ask children to create sounds through easily available objects, such as rice or pebbles in containers, using spoons to make the clip-clop sound, or even just clapping their hands. Another story that explores language and can use musical instruments is Michael Rosen's *We're Going on a Bear Hunt*.

Use finger puppets to help tell the story.

Developing a story's plot line through the use of character finger puppets helps children understand the basics of storytelling. The use of the puppets adds more dimension to the storytelling session. Through movement children actively

Wordless Books for Primary Students
- *Changes, Changes* by Pat Hutchins
- *Frog Goes to Dinner* by Mercer Mayer
- *Picnic* by Emily Arnold McCully
- *The Red Book* by Barbara Lehman
- *Tuesday* by David Wiesner

engage in the session. Providing gestural movement for a puppet adds to the fun. Creating a voice and making choices using the puppet's gestural actions all contribute to the story's retelling. Playmaking with puppets makes the storytelling more experiential and will aid the children in remembering the details in the plot, which is helpful with the retelling of traditional tales. The puppets can be as simple as character pictures from comic books, catalogues, or even computer-generated illustrations, all cut out and attached to Popsicle sticks. Basic illustrations, such as the sun, clouds, a forest, or a house, will help dramatize the story setting in an active playmaking session.

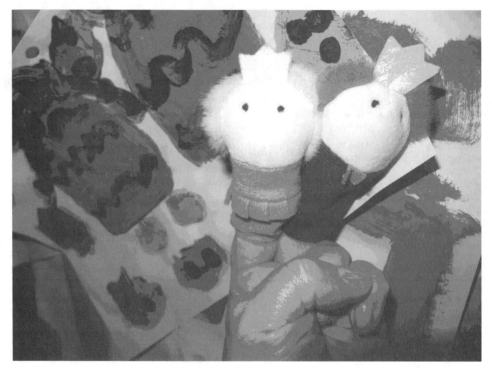

These simple puppets establish character gender and royal blood. The child art helps create the setting for storytelling.

Showing understanding through storytelling

One of the reasons we teach children about story structures and the importance of language is in the hope that they will eventually be able to share their own experiences of learning. Telling a story is their way of showing understanding of and interpreting what they know. For children to become effective speakers, we first need to pique their interest in expressing ideas and narratives they know something about. Asking children to share aloud their own cultural traditions and family stories will help them appreciate the value of oral traditions. When we build an oral storytelling culture with children, we can expect them to value hearing stories shared through speech.

Asking Questions about Story Play

Children often play out a story through improvised play that allows them to explore the many possibilities of story. Asking questions will help build their oral language skills and how they can bring new information to their version of the story. For example, a Kindergarten teacher, Leslie, asked these questions of children after reading an exciting fantasy story.

Leslie: Tell me, Liam, why is the dragon sleeping?

Liam: Because . . . because he is pooped after doing all of that flying around the room.

Leslie: What do you think he should do when he wakes up?

Kate: He should say he is sorry to the princess.

Leslie: How might he do that?

Using key questions such as *who, what, where, when,* and *why* will help children generate more details from the plot. This creative thought process, stimulated by asking many different kinds of questions as a part of the story-making session, helps children learn that story is built on many imaginative possibilities. Improvising scenes of what could happen beyond the plot will prompt children to use their imaginations and creativity. Your questions during play in a story structure activity will help children to share what they know about the story and to expand upon these ideas through improvisation.

The Importance of Play in the Development of Oral Language

Oral language is central to the early literacy development of children. The stronger the oral language base, the better the reading foundation. If we encourage children to explore and make new discoveries using talking, as well as learning through play centres and other scenarios outlined in this chapter, we will ultimately help them to understand how the functions, form, and content of the language they use to communicate are important. Playing with language builds a platform upon which children learn to decode words. When teachers build expressive language through active listening and play-based activities, it encourages students to ask questions and listen to answers in contexts that are familiar to them.

The explanations of how oral language develops, the play vignettes, and the planning for talk and storytelling contained in this chapter all encourage teachers to build their students' knowledge base and confidence about how to use language to communicate effectively. Children come to know that words, how they are used, and the gestures paired with them may not be appropriate in every situation. Teachers often have a vital role in helping children make all of these connections. Most important, by playfully encouraging children to think about the ways in which they speak, teachers build bridges to the more complex reading and writing tasks encountered in later grades.

"True play is spontaneous and uncertain — you never know where it will take you."
— Carl Honoré, *Under Pressure: Rescuing Childhood from the Culture of Hyper-parenting*

3

Understanding Print through Play: Towards Reading and Writing

Even before they come to school, most children know that oral language can be represented through symbols and marks on a page. Through the observation of language in use around them — environmental print — children come to understand that language appears in many forms. Children who are immersed in play-based environments can experiment with how language is used, constructing an understanding about the forms of written language, their meanings, and the connections between them. This is how they come to understand that the marks on a page have meaning in and of themselves.

Classrooms that are play oriented allow time for children to experiment with and experience language, but achieving this can be a challenge for many school curriculums, which call for children to do skill-based worksheets. Many worksheets ask children to practise needed skills, such as printing and making numbers. While we agree that these skills are needed, we also know that asking children to learn and practise skills in isolation from an active engagement with language may make it harder for them to see the connection between what they are doing and language in use. Understanding through play how their everyday language is used builds needed foundations for reading and writing.

Immersion in Print and Social Interaction

Many language theorists have clearly demonstrated that children come to language use when they are immersed in a print and verbally rich environment that encourages interaction (Dyson, 2003; Graves, 1994; Hall, 1987; Heath, 1983). In an enriched environment, children learn the important and needed aspects of language, including the differences between language and sound, the rules that govern its use, its varying meanings, and how to use it.

So, make sure that your environment is print rich. Recently, I visited a Grade 2 classroom, where the teacher had placed labels on things so that children would be accustomed to the use of words with objects to see how words can represent their visual knowledge of the world. Taking this approach is an important way to include children whose home language is other than English — show their first language words, as well. Be careful, however, not to perpetuate visual noise in the classroom.

Taking attendance each morning is important as children begin to realize that they are accountable — that they are at school to learn! Asking children to sign in on a daily sheet reminds them of the importance of their names. They may find it motivational to view how others write their names and form letters. Using the attendance list to reinforce who is in school reminds children that print has a function in sharing news or knowledge in the world.

Although providing a print-rich environment will encourage language learning, children's interaction is what brings rich language learning. In other words, children need good language modeling by others; however, if they are to become literate, they also need to experiment and test out different hypotheses on how language works.

We know from research in children's play that the building of language ability and skills happens when children interact with one another through play. In her studies conducted in Israel and the United States, Sara Smilansky (1990) found that dramatic play and socio-dramatic play both contribute to the development of cognitive and socio-emotional skills in young children. The children in Smilansky's studies showed many gains in school literacy as a result of their play: these included richer vocabulary, higher language comprehension, more curiosity about language, and better verbalization.

The key element — and the one that does so much good during play episodes — is that the situation almost always requires children to talk to one another. Children regularly come up with interesting themes and locations for their play, such as going to the doctor, visiting the vet's office, or running a café. Agreed-upon themes, such as "let's play restaurant" or "let's play school," can become the common ground for collaborative playmaking. As they play out scenarios, children describe what they are doing and show how everyday objects can symbolize other things. Basically, free play encourages risk taking through the sharing of children's ideas about what to play. Playmaking draws from the pretend world and grows within the frames of a specific theme.

Constructive play lends opportunity for the teacher to support students' language interaction. In many ways, this is a perfect type of interaction for children, one where they can, at the same time, gain confidence and regulate themselves in language ability. Imagine a trio of children getting ready to put on a rock concert: they might be practising with their instruments, drawing up pretend tickets, or trying out dance moves — this sort of play invites the teacher to expand on what children know and scaffold in new learning by asking critical questions and providing resources.

Children's functional play contributes in the same way to their emergent literacy in writing. It may be witnessed in the early classroom Writing Centre, where children practise writing their names and those of their peers. These pretend-written forms may be letters to relatives, complete with invented spelling, or message pads filled with imaginary messages for friends. As opposed to other sorts of playing, sending notes, drawing pictures, and making lists are all writing-practice play scenarios, efforts that build towards real writing engagements. At first, such attempts may have just simple symbols to characterize letters and words, but as children notice how letters are formed and how print is used to communicate, they begin to use real letters from the alphabet to convey their meanings to others.

> **Following Games with Rules**
>
> Games with rules are particularly helpful when we are teaching children English language forms. Just as the games require a certain narrow interpretation of rules, so does English sometimes require a more concrete learning process. When playing games governed by rules, such as board games, children have to understand how to use language forms just to get through them. Just as important, however, they must know how to interpret the rules of the game and negotiate with others. Children begin to associate the rules of a given board game as a guiding form to find success.

Environmental Print — Reading Our World

Environmental print is the print we see in our everyday world. It is the forms of language that have meaning in our environment. Sometimes called "directional print," or "signage," it is children's first reading experience of the world around them. Environmental print could be television/VCR buttons, street signs, logos, newspaper ads, notices, magazines, notes, food packages, and catalogues.

Most children quickly come to see how environmental print symbols represent meaning. To offer a common example, many children understand street signs, like WALK or STOP, long before they comprehend any conventional text. Connecting children's first reading to environmental print also builds confidence, competence with language, and self-esteem. Most children can also readily connect meaning to environmental print, as early reading experiences have already occurred in the home and in their community.

One pioneer researcher in early literacy, Marie Clay (1993), found that children often first become engaged in reading environmental print. In a study she established that children explore varying aspects of print in the home and surrounding community. Early engagements in reading include the reading of signs, cereal boxes, and commercials — and children's interest in books and print emerges as a result of these early connections. Children begin to form hypotheses about how letters form words and words lead to messages of communication.

Children often play-make meaning using the print they see. Not long ago, I watched a group of preschool children make tickets for a community hockey game that was raising money for a hospital. One boy had a sibling with cystic fibrosis, and visiting the hospital was a common experience for him when home with his mom. Excitedly and making use of the boy's experience, the children designed what they thought the ticket should look like. This artifact showed much literacy understanding, evoking both the hospital and the hockey game. The boy had tangential experience of both, enough to create a graphic impression, even though his command of real print was slight.

Often, when children enter school, parents feel as if the literacy experiences they have had may not be what is needed in school. In a session I conducted on school readiness, a mother shared this: "I am afraid we don't read to our daughter enough. Kayla can't really spell anything, and she never plays with the word-builder game we bought. She will be way behind the others!" In reality, her child was neither behind nor ahead of the rest of the children in emergent literacy. The mother was following the typical popular culture message about literacy, which suggests that only conventional reading of narrative texts is literacy. I tried to reassure her that her daughter was coming to understand printed text in a perfectly adequate fashion and that her overall environment was fine.

In an overview of language and literacy in the early years, Terry Piper (2003) presented several factors related to preschool learning to consider when children enter the formalized instruction of the classroom. Children grow and come to language at different stages; their readiness for more formalized learning varies. Many children have a sense of what interests them and what does not. Their experiences of play have an impact on their language ability — social interaction is central to their language and literacy learning.

One useful tool we have is the ability to make students excited and curious about their world by introducing them to printed text that matters in how they read their world. As children enter the classroom door, the onus is on us to find out what children can do and what they find challenging. By beginning literacy engagements for children with what they already know, we can empower them to include the learning they bring to the classroom. Unless parents have made concerted efforts to avoid consumer products (and even then), children often know a number of logos and corporate symbols, such as the McDonald's golden arches, grocery items such as Froot Loops, Kraft Macaroni and Cheese, and store names, such as Toys "R" Us. (Children not raised in North America, however, may find these symbols and print quite foreign; in that situation, it may be useful to ask parents to situate your understanding of what early print exposure would have represented in their first countries.)

Harste, Burke, and Woodward (1984) looked at early literacy development and print awareness. In their study they found that children know a lot about print before formalized instruction begins, but early language programs often assume that children know little about it. Their study had interesting implications for teachers, in that early-grade educators would have greater success in promoting print awareness if they built on the many language strategies and knowledge that children have about print before they enter the classroom. The researchers also argued that children need to learn written language in a variety of experiences, especially those that are representative of the world in which they live. Most important, the researchers concluded that children acquire language ability through a whole language approach.

Classroom Ideas for Exploring Environmental Print

Below are some common scenarios presented with an emphasis on fostering awareness of environmental print.

The imaginary restaurant

This scenario can be played out in different ways, depending on what the teacher hopes to achieve. When the goal is to focus on environmental print, then do the following:

- Collect a variety of restaurant and other take-out menus, or ask the children to bring them in. Aim to represent a wide variety of cuisine choices (e.g., Indian, Chinese, and Italian).
- Prompt the children to either draw or cut out photos of the foods represented, or find or create pictures of their favorites.
- Invite the children to either use the existing menus or create their own.

With menus in hand, the children can role-play a variety of café and restaurant scenarios. Since the goal here is to create awareness of print, if the play can be extended, it should lean towards print activities, such as creating snack labels, posters for imaginary restaurants, snacking guides, and simple recipes.

The local landmark alphabet book

A landmark alphabet book, based on the children's own community, is a good way to encourage both print awareness and local connectedness.

- Ask parents to help children obtain local tourist information and publications, postcards, and maps, and to share photographs that they may have in family photo collections.
- Encourage the children to identify landmarks that are important to them, perhaps parks, a library, or a church.

Each landmark should be assigned a letter and then represented either by a drawn picture, a photograph, or one of the gathered printed sources. Eventually, these can be combined into an alphabet book.

This play could be extended by changing some of the letters to correspond to seasonal variations in the environment, such as showing the landmark in both a winter and a summer setting. Another idea is to focus on one landmark and engage in a wider exploration of it, say, the history and environment of a popular local park.

Postcards from far away

This game requires advance planning and the cooperation of parents and other adults, but it can be satisfying and interesting for children. The idea is to make geography more real by bringing a personal experience to the mystery of Somewhere Else.

In essence, the children are encouraged to have parents, friends, and relatives who travel or live away to send postcards to the classroom or to return with them to the classroom. Depending on who can be persuaded to send them, these postcards can be displayed on a map of the country or even of the world.

Another variation is to get the class to create their own postcards, based on either real places you have studied or on imaginary places they have envisioned. These can then be filled in and "mailed" within the school.

Either activity can be combined with classroom map-making. These maps can be as simple as showing the way from the child's home to a park, or from school to home. Rather than drawing the spaces to which the map reader is to be guided, ask children to cut out representative pictures from magazines and catalogues. For example, a tree can represent a park, or a car, a parking lot.

Bridging Children's Home and School Worlds

Environmental print is being used to bridge the gap between home and school in Jenny Temple's classroom. In her early literacy intervention program, she uses a number of language representations to help the class create an ABC book. A part of this program involves parents helping build skills at home. Using objects from children's neighborhood, homes, and schools, Jenny actively involves her students as she connects their cultural and learning worlds.

Jenny initially asked parents to bring in their children's favorite books; however, she quickly noted that some did not have any books. Instead, when parents visited the classroom, Jenny chatted about reading in an environmental fashion. She offered grocery flyers, catalogues, and coupons she had received in her own mailbox, and explained how these accessible resources could be used in a casual fashion to reinforce print recognition. Parents were pleased to discover that everyday print is one of the best ways to introduce children to early concepts of print — many of these parents had had difficulty with school as children, while others were newcomers learning English.

Sources of Environmental Print
- Newspapers
- Community event pamphlets
- Calendars
- Advertisements
- Recipes
- Restaurant menus
- Junk mail
- Street signs
- Food cartons/Product containers

Using Environmental Print

- Use environmental print to promote a talk curriculum. Provide a list of environmental print items, such as the one at left, and make it available for parents to help children collect items. Ask children to describe how they came upon items and to share their experiences. As a group, you could create a scrapbook of children's literacy experiences to show how home and school together can become a learning community.
- Teach letters and words in contexts that define a child's world. Use sheets of logos that can be accessed from the Internet. Doing this can help children to understand that letters make up words.
- Active engagement in reading helps children to understand that as you do, you become. In other words, asking children to contribute print examples from their environment to form a personal ABC book promotes literacy in their world.

While educators are called upon to make use of environmental print, it is just as important that parents take the same opportunities. Homes are filled with numerous printed artifacts, all of which can be introduced to children in a playful fashion. I recommend that, in a light-hearted and amusing fashion, parents use these environmental artifacts to encourage their children's emergent literacy.

Ideas to pass on to parents are presented as a line master on the next page.

Language Development through Dramatic Play

One of the primary ways in which playful learning is achieved is through a rich interactive curriculum, one in which children's interactions with each other and the environment all generate talking — and nothing encourages talking among young children more than dramatic play. From our own childhoods, we probably remember teachers trying to get us to stop talking. For younger children, talk is an essential part of their learning. Deciding what the pretend play will be requires discussion, collaborative meaning making, and problem solving. The drama often depends on children directly sharing what they are doing and how particular objects will serve as needed props to move the scenario forward. The drama is created from within the children's imaginative play and the talk that frames the scenario.

Ideas for Promoting Early Literacy with Your Children

Make literacy engagements with print a part of your home and family routine.

- Engage your children in helping to write a grocery list. Write the items down in a numbered list and ask them to help by copying letters. As they print the name of an item such as "milk," say the letters out loud: "m-i-l-k." Point to the letters of the word as you speak.
- Use your list as the basis for a scavenger hunt within the kitchen, and ask the children to help find the items on the list.
- Talk about how things are grouped — for example, cold things (e.g., meats and dairy products that go into the fridge) and canned and bagged food that may be kept in a cupboard. Doing this helps children to notice how we sort and classify items.
- Help your children to read their world, as well, by pointing out words and letters everywhere you can. Read traffic signs, billboards, logos, store signs, and more. Point out specific letters in each sign.
- Ask your children to begin naming common signs and to find some letters. While passing a McDonald's sign, for example, ask, "What letter does this word start with?"
- Ask your children to identify words and letters noticed while you are driving. For example, play I Spy while making obvious use of the alphabet so that they will look around the environment for something whose word begins with the asked-for letter.
- Ask guiding questions to engage children in conversations that promote early literacy awareness:
  1. How do you know that says "Skittles"? How do you know that says "Walmart"?
  2. What letter do you see at the beginning?
  3. What sound does the letter *S* make?
  4. Do you recognize any other letters in that logo?
  5. Can you find another logo that begins with the same letter?
  6. Do those words begin with the same sound?
  7. Are any of those letters in your own name?

Helpful websites for encouraging literacy skills

Used in moderation and with parental supervision, sites such as these can provide a constructive supplement to efforts such as those outlined above. As with all things Web related, first explore any site thoroughly. Ensure that the content is positive and that games are age appropriate.

- Click on a letter in the alphabet to see a picture of that letter and hear its sounds.
  http://www.learningplanet.com/act/fl/aact/alphastart.swf
- Check out the Children's Digital Library.
  http://www.storyplace.org/
- This site helps to inspire a love of reading and writing.
  http://www.starfall.com/
- Enjoy games, coloring, videos, and music, and visit sites about the child's favorite cartoon characters! Visits help children learn letters, build words, make sentences, and expand vocabulary.
  http://pbskids.org/
- The website of the popular educational TV show offers many simple and interesting games that take a basic look at letters, words, and numbers.
  http://www.sesamestreet.org/home

In Susan's Grade 1 class, during the playtime that comes immediately after lunch, several girls began a discussion about a popular TV show, which featured teenagers winning a talent contest. Susan observed them quietly and quickly realized that none of them had seen the show in question but had heard enough about it to be interested.

Cherrise, one of the class leaders, began organizing the play.

Cherrise: Let's put on our own show. I want to be the judge.

Tani: I want to be a judge too — the one who always says bad stuff!

Kayla: I want to be on it . . . I'm going to sing. (*She gestures as a singer with microphone.*)

Cherrise: Let's make the cards. . . . We'll give out points. Let's make the cards.

Sam: Okay. Wait. We need a band like on the show. I will play the drums. We need more —.

Mark: (*interrupting*) I want to be the host. I will call people out to the stage.

The discussion continued, as the girls happily organized the talent show. Other children became involved, as well. Susan noticed that no one performed anything — they had too much fun chatting while they organized and reorganized their show.

In the feature below, Dr. Toni Doyle, a reading professor, discusses the connection between literacy and talk in and about play-acting.

The Literacy Connection and Play

To the observer of young children playing in the classroom, there is no doubt that, during play, children are freed from their normal roles and step into a space in which the exploration of new identities and interactions are welcomed. They are free to explore new ideas and use language to represent these ideas in ways that reality-based activities do not permit. When children play, whether through story re-enactments or socio-dramatic play — play in which children act out real-life situations such as "playing house" or "playing school"— they talk about the course that the play will take. In the Kindergarten classroom, the observer can watch the children constructing the setting, characters, and plot lines — formulating ideas, discussing these, and accepting and rejecting the play scenario that is to unfold — both before and during the play episode.

Some researchers suggest that this type of talk about play — referred to as "metaplay" — is an indicator of children's ability to think about language and is associated with children's later reading and writing success. Because these activities provide unique opportunities for children to engage in language that is play specific and, therefore, not usually heard or used in other daily experiences, play is an important component in the design of the instructional environment. Play resources, including space, props, and "dress-up" clothes, combined with unobtrusive guidance by the teacher "to get things going," help to ensure that the opportunities for learning through play are maximized.

— Dr. Toni Doyle

Dramatic play allows children to develop vocabulary and appropriate situational behavior. Teachers can encourage this development by helping students to use language appropriate for a given play scenario. For example, if the children are playing Restaurant, then there should be a play menu, a chef, named food items, and so on.

When the play scenarios are predetermined, teachers may prepare vocabulary lists and place them in the appropriate play centres. For Dentist's Office, for example, you would probably want words for x-rays, toothbrushes, waiting room, and the dentist's chair. The more vocabulary you introduce, the more children will likely enjoy being immersed in the play, and the more opportunities they will have to use and learn new words.

Dramatic play encourages experimentation with language and promotes the understandings that letters become words and that written language lends opportunity for them to be seen as writers. Dramatic play scenarios should provide many chances for reading and writing, even if the use of these skills is imaginary or rudimentary. The goal is to create an environment where these uses can later be turned into something real. Just like any skill, emergent literacy requires a background — dramatic role-play can help provide it.

Although the students may come up with interesting play scenarios, teachers have the opportunity to encourage a wide variety of scenarios. Teachers should change the centres or play scenarios frequently, and encourage all the students to assume different roles. Some scenarios may become quite elaborate and involve large groups of children. This is fine, as long as all the children participate. It is recommended that students spend 20 to 30 minutes exploring, experiencing, and sharing what they know in any role-play scenario.

Teachers need to create time and space in their classrooms for role-play, not only to help students practise their oral language and written skills, but to do much more. Dramatic play is both fun and interesting to children. When it is combined with other classroom goals, both the learning and the teaching improve.

Some classrooms sequester dramatic play into centres, or special corners, where props, objects, and dress-up items spark the imagination. Everyone has seen make-believe kitchens, a popular feature in waiting rooms where children are likely to congregate. Such centres do not require elaborate and expensive toys. Instead, they provide a safe and secure space in which imagination is encouraged to take hold, and objects are ready at hand to assume whatever role is necessary for them.

It is important that teachers help the children understand how dramatic play and a dramatic play centre works. Some children will already know, but others will hardly understand where to start. At first, the teacher can even join in the game. Below, Grade 1 teachers Nancy Pelley and Debbie Toope describe a literacy learning event that points to the value of dramatic play.

> "We can play house and pretend we are the mommy and daddy."
> — Child (age 5)

Supporting Critical Literacy through Role Play

In our Grade 1 classroom, we were studying the genre of fairy tales. Our read-alouds included many different versions of the same fairy tale, as well as fractured fairy tales. We began by using puppets and face masks as props, and children worked in small groups to retell their favorite tales through dramatic play. As children became comfortable with this medium of representation, they began taking control of the play by reinventing and dramatizing various fairy tales, making creative changes.

One group of children dramatized the fairy tale "Snow White and the Seven Dwarfs." In listening to their dialogue, I [Nancy] observed how they had become critical in their analysis of the fairy tale. They decided that Snow White would not have fallen for the stepmother's trick the second time and would have refused the apple. They believed Snow White to be smart because she had persuaded the huntsman to free her and had survived in the woods alone until finding the dwarfs' home. In their representation of the fairy tale, they re-created the scene by changing the ending to suit their analysis.

Another group of children represented the fairy tale "Cinderella." As they dialogued through interactive play, they decided that Cinderella would not want to marry the prince because she did not want to belong to anyone. They decided that having looked after her stepmother and step sisters, she would rather be free. In their dramatization, they reinvented the ending to suit their view of the world: Cinderella thanked the prince for finding her lost slipper and then asked her fairy godmother to lock up her stepsisters. She lived happily ever after alone in her father's house.

— Nancy Pelley and Debbie Toope

Dramatic Play Centres

"Having mark-making tools that are easily accessible and able to cross boundaries of play centres is key to inspiring these creative experiences."
— Dr. Tara-Lynn Scheffel

Piaget (1962) argued that children use symbolic play to better understand their life experiences. Through dramatic play children try to understand the nature of their world. Essentially, they rehearse their future roles in life. When reinforced with appropriate props, a dramatic play centre can help children to use and expand their imaginations, to build upon, dramatize, and be part of that created world.

Teachers facilitate early literacy when they interact in dramatic play centres. Dramatic play offers many possibilities for children to see how literacy informs their lives. Teachers may enter in-role as participants or as facilitators offering an opportunity to explore language in a number of forms. They can help develop children's literacy through asking questions, suggesting problem solving to a dramatic play scenario, and modeling the different functions of print in each of the centres.

Suggested on the next few pages are a few of the many types of centres that can be created to permit children to rehearse life experiences — these are intended to be open entry and open-ended.

Eye doctor centre

Check with parents to see if they have any old doctor or nurse sets at home. Collect small containers with lids and plastic sunglasses. Set a small table in front of a corner in the classroom, and place items in which children can record things: an appointment book, a calendar, and a number of clipboards with information cards that children may complete. Provide a number of chairs and books for children to read, as they wait for their appointment. Make a simple eye chart and other charts that have letter blends and words for the week. Pop one of the plastic lenses out of the sunglasses, so that children may safely test their vision and word knowledge with just one eye. Create note pads for doctor prescriptions. Always encourage the children to take turns role-playing: patient, receptionist, nurse, and eye doctor.

Museum centre

To role-play using the theme of a museum, children need to understand what museums are and what their purpose is. Museum is an excellent centre and an inspiring play scenario when paired with a field trip to a museum. A role-play museum needs a theme that the children can contribute to and that relates to what the class is exploring, for example, birds, shapes, a form of transportation, or even individual letters.

What works really well is using a shoebox. Involve the children in groups or individually in making their own displays of artifacts or pictures and treating shoeboxes as display cabinets. All items displayed should have a label. For the letter idea, for example, ask children to share objects with the sound or spelling. Having children make a listing of their artifacts with a picture of each teaches classifying and sorting skills. Display the shoeboxes for a parent night or at an annual literacy fair.

Growing, or garden, centre

Creating a growing centre for children, whether in your classroom or outside, is a rewarding and holistic activity that connects children with their world. The life cycle of a plant is a popular unit in the early years. Bring in seedling growing trays, and introduce children to the idea of planting a garden. Letting the children choose and plant seeds is a great way for them to understand the life cycle of a plant. Plants are observed for size, color, and texture, as children follow a step-by-step procedure. Children can be involved in spotting words on seed packs and in reading and writing plant labels.

Creating a buying area with plastic plant pots in a range of sizes, catalogues for ordering plants, and garden furniture could be an extension of the garden. Children can make their own seed packs by cutting envelopes in half. Ask children to represent language in many forms from drawing pictures of the plant, to writing names and prices of seeds. As a class, write down the growing instructions, and have children copy them onto packages. Provide a shoebox where the seed envelopes could be kept according to the type (e.g., tomato, peppers, beans). Provide checklists with boxes where children can check off what they are purchasing, the number of each, and the cost. In this way children can learn about graphing and mathematics.

Café/Restaurant centre

Creating a role-play café lends opportunity to celebrate the many cultures you may have in your classroom. Decide together on the types of food to place on the menu, and invite children to share their cultural practices. In one Grade 1 classroom I visited, the teacher had found pictures of the varying cultural foods children had chosen for the menu and created the children's menu with these pictures. Parents were thrilled to see how she had included aspects of their cultural heritage, and the children learned implicit lessons about diversity. This role-play offers a great opportunity to extend a unit on holidays and celebrations in a tangible way.

Ask for children's help in creating the café. They can bring in plastic cutlery, paper or plastic plates, cups, and bowls. At the same time, you can collect safe plastic cutlery, plates, cups, and bowls. Set up tables and seats, create order pads, perhaps find or make a phone, and place a toy cash register at the front of the restaurant. This centre encourages children's emergent literacy, as they can write in many forms ranging from the menu and price labels to posters and the sign for their café.

Pet hospital

Ask children to bring in a stuffed animal from home to serve as a pet. Ideally, a variety of animals will be represented. Make a list of animal types, for example, dog, cat, snake, and fish. Provide a registration sheet where they can answer simple questions about their pets. Using cardboard boxes, ask the children to prepare carrying crates for their animals and to provide items that help meet the basic needs of their pets. Provide a uniform for the vet and assistant. Talk with students about how to watch out for pets' safety and health. For a unit on people in our community, invite an animal technician to come and show the students how to safely hold and care for their pets, and to talk about the types of medical attention that animals receive at a veterinarian's office. Have children record on a clipboard and paper their care of the animals during their visit.

In the feature below, Kindergarten teacher Liz Macintosh shares and reflects on a group experience of imaginative play in her classroom.

Imaginative Play: Getting Ready for Scorpion Island

One day I happened to notice that the boys in my class were quite busy. They were engaged in conversation and moving around the classroom. I wanted to find out what they were doing without intruding on their play activity. I overheard them talking about wanting to go to a place called "Scorpion Island." They had divided themselves into two teams and written up member lists for these teams. They even drew maps of the island and discussed among themselves how to reach this magical place. Totally engrossed in their activity, they were imagining the things they would encounter on the island and the supplies they would need for their trip. The experience was real and meaningful to them.

— Liz Macintosh

Centre for tourism workers and travel agents

For this centre, drop by a travel agent's office and collect some brochures, posters, and pictures about holiday adventures. Encourage the children to note the different places in the world they could visit and to make their own posters and brochures. Set out a number of desks and ask children to make nameplates and business cards. Provide a holiday adventure form that asks for simple information, such as type of travel and destination. Invite children to seek out informational books from the library, to find out more about a destination. Globes and atlases help children to situate particular places. As children book their imaginary holidays, place a small pin or marker on the map. Prepare holiday booking forms, asking children to fill in customer name, destination, and how they want to travel. Discuss the roles to be played, such as tourist, person who books the trips, and tour guide. A further extension could be for children to create an imaginary scrapbook of where they journeyed.

This is a great centre and play scenario to help children understand the world in which we live and to raise cultural awareness of the different countries children may come from. It is also a wonderful centre to include within a unit on transportation.

A Junior Kindergarten student has created a passport for use at the centre for tourism and travel.

Television news show

Centres that promote children's language use and play can also be developed on the following themes:
• Garage
• Movie theatre
• Bakery
• Supermarket

The fact that television is likely to be a significant part of your students' lives makes it an ideal candidate for a role-play or centre. Use a desk for the TV anchor. Encourage the students to write simple news stories, based on school and community events. They can imitate graphics by making posters and can create weather maps. Have the students take turns in different roles, including news anchor, reporter, cameraperson, and director. Other students can role-play interview subjects. If time and technology allow, record the news show and play it later as classroom entertainment.

Active Engagement with Words and Letters

Teaching children to read and write is about creating a small series of links and building blocks between sounds, symbols, and eventually words and sentences. One of the first and most important links is connecting the letter they already know verbally to the visual representation of that letter, and then helping them to sound out the word, with a focus on the initial letter.

One important theme of this book is that children must make meaning by reading the world around them; that said, the curriculum demands they also grasp the basic tenets of letter formation. Using read-alouds, where the teacher engages the children in listening and discussion, is a way to point out certain features of print to children along with the connections of letters to the associated sounds. Looking at alphabet books and connecting each letter to its visual form and helping them to sound out a word with a focus on the initial letter are the beginning links for reading.

We want children to build understanding about their world and to use the associated language to make more observations. Using concept books to engage children in discussions about the alphabet and associated letter vocabulary introduces the understandings of the functions of print. Children can see the use of both upper- and lower-case letters and how the corresponding illustration of the letter contributes to their association of a letter to a corresponding object or concept. Concept books are of particular importance because they explore complex ideas, such as telling time, classifying, and sorting — thereby orienting children to our world. In particular, many concept books, such as alphabet books, centre on culture and customs, which also helps children to acknowledge and accept all cultures and practices.

Writing in all forms, even simple ones, can and should be incorporated into the play areas of the classroom. Even young children use a combination of symbols and letters to engage the beginnings of print knowledge. For example, labels made to direct children where to place things are important. To use some of the play scenarios described earlier: A container at the eye doctor's could be labeled "Pencils"; at the travel agency, a box could be labeled "Forms." These things help children to focus on how we use letters to "name" things.

Class routines, such as these, offer many opportunities to introduce letter forming.

- During the morning message, whereby children gather at the front of the class as the first activity of the day, the teacher can create a name guessing game: "I would like this helper to come forward: she has an S at the beginning of her name and it has an /S/ sound as in 'snake.'" The teacher then makes the letter formation in the air.
- Another effort involves creating stations where students explore the formation of letters, as well as how they can connect letters to words in their names.
- Pass around a class list, with all their names printed in large bold letters. Ask each student to circle the focus letter in her or his name or in the name of a friend.

As children learn more letters and symbols, they should be encouraged to use and incorporate these into their early writings. Teachers should always be involved, in order to scaffold children's imaginative play to written letters and symbols.

Play with names

One of the best ways to start connecting sounds to letters is via children's own names, among the first words they hear and the first words they see written out many times. Sometimes, children will begin with just the first letter: "Look, there's an *S*, like me, Sam. . . ." From there they begin to recognize other letters in their names, gradually making the connections between those letters, the sounds they make, and their names in a textual form. The first step, however, is to ensure that children recognize their names. Choose a consistent way of using each name, spelled and pronounced the same way it is used in the home.

A number of simple games using the child's own name will reinforce the link between letters and sounds, and, depending on the child's name, encourage an early understanding of phonics and spelling. Some of these will encourage

"It is hard to know what moments the child remembers in the future, but teaching the child to write his or her name is an amazing experience. The joy for both child and teacher is something that I will always remember."
— Nina Fullbrook, Early Years' Teacher

children to recognize their names and the constituent letters, while others will develop their letter–sound linkages a little further.

In the opening days of school, teachers may want to take the following playful approach to having students learn the names of their classmates and how to pronounce the names correctly.

Resources: Manila and construction paper, scissors, glue, crayons, pencils

- Ask students to print their first and last names in capital letters on stiff paper, name-tag size. Provide cutouts of unusual shapes (e.g., hearts or hexagons), and ask the children to glue them to a piece of colored construction paper. Do the same with your name.
- Collect the name tags and place them in a box. Have students take turns drawing a name tag from the box, finding the child who owns it, and pronouncing the name correctly. The child (or teacher) whose name tag is drawn will determine if the pronunciation is correct. The whole class should then repeat the name in unison.

Suggestions that apply most to the home are presented as a line master for parents on the next page.

Developmental Stages of Writing

Children's writing development is characterized by six stages. Writing begins with a basic exploration of marks on the page and then zigzags until it becomes an entrenched practice with the child producing actual letters to form words and sentences.

1. *Drawing:* Regardless of skill, all children should be encouraged to draw. It will develop physical comfort with tools like pencils, but it will also create an awareness of the skill — representing something real via a graphic on a page.
2. *Scribbling, random and controlled:* First attempts at writing often result in scribbling or other drawings that are purely abstract. As time goes by, these scribbles become more concrete and begin to resemble something. Often, the child will establish the difference, dismissing one piece of "art" as scribbling while describing another as a letter to Grandma, even though the parent or educator would be hard-pressed to make any distinction.
3. *Forms that resemble letters:* From scribbling, children progress to letter forms that demonstrate a clear attempt at printing. While the results are likely to be mixed and inconsistent, the educator will usually be able to recognize the child's intentions.
4. *Letters that are recognizable:* At first, these are likely to vary widely in shape, construction, and size, with adherence to a line being optional. As time goes by and the child gains more skill, the patterns will get more consistent and the results more frequently recognizable.
5. *Spelling:* The child begins putting letters and groups of letters into sounds. Again, this process is gradual. At first the child will probably just guess, attaching a familiar sound to a spelling. As the child's skill base widens, he or she will be able to spell words with more alacrity.
6. *Words and sentences:* The conclusion of this process is the ability to print recognizable words and sentences, with the appropriate punctuation.

Name Games and Activities

Home provides many opportunities for parents to help their children learn their names. Here are some ideas to put into practice:

- Spell the child's name when you use it; talk about the sounds and the letters.

- Label some of your child's possessions, and put a nameplate on the bedroom door, so he or she sees the name used as a printed text.

- Encourage the child to sign cards and letters, even if the printing is unclear.

- Cut out letters from advertisements and catalogues, and encourage your child to use them to spell his or her name. Do the same with alphabet blocks or fridge letters.

- Ask your child to identify the letters in her or his name within the environment — look at billboards, mail, menus, and so on. If your child finds this too hard, just focus on the first letter in the name.

- Tell stories that use the child's name instead of that of the main character, and spell out the name whenever possible.

- Make a photo album with the child, and label the photographs:
  "Ashley playing soccer"
  "Ashley in her Halloween costume."
  Ask your child questions that will elicit answers about what is happening in the photos.

- Invite your child to work with baking and cooking ingredients, such as rice and flour, on cookie sheets to practise making letters.

- From a nature walk, you may find items such as pebbles and sticks; your child can then use these to practise constructing his or her name.

- When shopping, ask your child to help locate letters of the alphabet that you see on labels and on signs.

- Every name is selected for a reason that becomes a part of someone's identity — perhaps a child is named after a beloved grandparent, for example. Explain that reason to help your child appreciate the importance of her or his name.

Below, teacher Karen Keogh shares her success with the Flat Stanley Project, a proven way to promote writing and reading among young children.

The Flat Stanley Project

One of the most fun, hands-on, play-based activities I have ever been involved in uses a paper doll to stimulate curiosity, creativity, oral and writing skills, problem solving, family involvement, imagination, journal writing, and illustrating. In Jeff Brown's story *Flat Stanley*, a little boy gets flattened by a bulletin board and ends up as thin as a piece of paper. He discovers that he can slide under doors, becomes a kite, and catches museum thieves by posing as a picture. Best of all, he can fit into an envelope and travel all over the world. A teacher in London, Ontario, Dale Hubert, developed the idea of having children write and illustrate their own versions of Flat Stanley's story as a way of improving their writing.

Each child decides how Stanley will look. I've seen them with freckles, glasses, earrings, chains, tattoos and a variety of skin colors. The paper dolls are laminated in case someone wants to take him to swimming lessons. The places Stanley goes will depend on the interests of the child and their families — I have often had requests for an extra Stanley for a younger sibling who wants to be part of the project, or they make their own.

As with any assignment, family involvement varies, but we celebrate all of Stanley's adventures. First, we read *Flat Stanley* and brainstorm the things you could do if you were flat. The project's flexibility makes redirecting it to a theme or subject area suitable for any grade easy. One year I chose "Me and My Family" as a Kindergarten social studies unit — we can learn so much about other cultures, new places, traditions, customs, other people, and ourselves through the project.

I send home a note to parents telling them that their child is bringing home a guest for three weeks. Stanley is learning all about real families and would like to be included in their daily lives. He doesn't eat much and can sleep on a bookshelf. Each child has a journal to record any three activities that the family does together. Children must include a brief description of the activity (helping to prepare a meal, going to church, playing board games, hiking, doing a puzzle, visiting Grandmother) and an illustration or photograph. Through stories, discussions, and visual literacy, my constant message to the children is that "there are different ways to be a family. Your family is special no matter what kind it is" (Parr, 2003). Parents often comment that they learn new things about their neighborhood, community, and province while showing Stanley around.

When the journals are completed, children share them with the class. The students talk about their favorite adventure and show their pictures. I also choose one page from each journal to make a class book that each child takes home to share with the family. As a teacher, I have a great deal of fun, too. I'll never forget the day the children came back from Music only to discover Stanley in their Easter baskets with chocolate all over his face. He was then called to the office by our principal for a time out because he took the chocolate eggs without asking!

In addition to going home with the children, Flat Stanley has had adventures overseas. He has visited many prominent members in our society as well as other countries. My Flat Stanley has seen a number of celebrities and media figures, all of whom sent back pictures of themselves with Stanley. He has visited New York, Hawaii, France, the Dominican Republic, India, Jamaica, and Italy. My class has often received postcards from Stanley when he goes on vacation, something that usually leads to an impromptu geography lesson complete with globe and a lively discussion about what Stanley might be doing, eating, and seeing. We also talk about our postal service and the steps involved in getting a postcard from Stanley to us. Every year, this activity snowballs and brings more fun and learning to my students.

The creativity involved is limited only by the imagination of the teacher and the students. For example, for Remembrance Day, we dressed extra Stanleys in camouflage and sent them to Afghanistan with messages for our troops.

— Karen Keough

For more information, see www.flatstanley.com.

"Play gives children a chance to practice what they are learning. . . . They have to play with what they know to be true in order to find out more and then they can use what they learn in new forms of play."
— Fred Rogers

Helping children's writing along

Making language real and writing authentic for children depends on children seeing how the task asked of them engages real communication. Providing authentic literacy experiences that frame their literacy engagements at home, such as going to the post office, the grocery store, subway stations, and restaurants, helps children see how written language is important to learn and use for communication with others. Modeling how to use telephone message pads, write grocery lists, and create recipes for a cooking session encourages children to use written forms in their play.

As children's scribbles begin to turn into real writing, there are a number of playful ways to lay down a foundation for their efforts and also promote a general awareness of writing in the world around them. On the next page are some games and exercises you can suggest that parents adopt to create this platform.

Promoting Literacy at Classroom Centres

Although infusing play-based centres with opportunities for children to use writing stimulates literacy learning, children also need more direct opportunities to learn about written language. Many early-grade classrooms have literacy centres that provide physical and temporal space for in-depth explorative play with language, in order to build the skills that will enable children to become competent communicators and language users. Oral sharing, reading aloud to children, and doing activities that use print to authenticate real-life experiences all happen at such centres. Literacy-related centres include the Book Centre, or classroom library and reading area, the Math Centre, the science and exploration table, and the Writing Centre.

Setting up the Book Centre

A centre or space devoted to books is important if we wish to create a reading culture with our young readers. It should be an especially inviting classroom area, a quiet, comfortable space in which to experience books. The centre is meant to have a cozy feel, to encourage quiet thought more than a frenzy of activity. Pillows, a centre rug, and small chairs can help create the feeling of a separate room, where children can go and have time to look at books.

Creating time with books allows children to see that books are to be valued. Exploring books on their own teaches them that reading is something they can

Encouraging Early Writing at Home

- Involve your child in your own writing: "Here is your grandmother's birthday card. Shall we write a little note before our names? We could say we hope all her birthday wishes come true."

- Encourage experimentation with pencils, pens, crayons, and paper. Many children like to imitate adult work. Pretend flow charts, instructions, and whatnot can all be created using nothing more than lined paper.

- Make a storybook together; have your child dictate the words and then watch you slowly and deliberately print the story out. Encourage your child to draw pictures and fill in what words he or she can.

- With your child, write letters to friends or relatives. The child should write as many letters as possible, and then dictate the rest.

- Encourage your child to take responsibility for household writing, even if the results are not ideal. Invite your child to sign cards, help draft lists, and make labels.

- Make a scrapbook or memory book that contains samples of your child's writing and art.

- Praise the effort, but not effusively. You want your child to learn that there is a right and a wrong approach to printing.

- Resist the temptation to take over or supervise too much when your child encounters trouble. Making mistakes is a huge part of this learning process.

- Play with toys and scenarios that involve writing, like writing pretend mail, making shopping lists, and filling in applications.

- Word Find is always a popular choice for learning letters and recognizing small words within larger words.

- Before taking a trip by car, train, or plane, discuss words associated with the trip, for example, luggage, map, gasoline, and trailer. Write out the words together.

- Look at newspapers and advertisements that come in the mail and ask your child to copy words that seem interesting.

- Supply paint, sand, shaving foam, or rice to encourage your child to play with letter formations.

- Play a game of letter jumble with magnetic letters on the fridge. Show one small word, such as "cat," and leave a group of letters nearby that could be used to create other words, for example, "m" for "mat."

- Reuse cardboard boxes, encouraging your child to build something like a robot. The new creation can be labelled and given a name, such as "Timmy the Robot."

do on their own. Picture books expand the imagination and can also connect children to other parts of the world.

Teachers, however, should interact with children in the Book Centre, to engage children in exploring age-appropriate books that span many genres, encompassing everything from fairy tales to nonfiction. Developing children's tastes for literature takes time. Many teachers read a wide variety of literature to their students.

Establishing book time

Organizing the reading experience by role-playing a library can be very interesting for the children. First, organize the books on a shelf, and use a desk for the checkout counter. Make up some cards for library borrowing. Display posters about books, or prompt the children to create ones for special events. Display a message board outside the mat area that today there will be a special visitor to the classroom.

In the role of a librarian, invite the children to the book time. Ask them to suggest how they could be a good audience for the reading. Present a reading in a specific genre or form of children's literature, such as fairy tales or concept books. Ask the children to check out their books before they begin to read. Involve them in selecting books for themed cardboard or plastic book boxes, such as rhymes, fairy tales, or books about animals. As children become more competent as readers, there can be a book talk, where a child takes on the role of the librarian and shares a book with the rest of the class. For older children, you can prompt reader response by asking for a simple review of one or two lines about why they liked or disliked a given book.

Choosing the books

See "Children's Books for Playful Learning," beginning on page 109, for a list of titles that can promote various kinds of learning, including talk, print knowledge, narrative understanding, and patterning.

Teachers need to select a variety of books likely to appeal to students of the diverse range of abilities and interests represented in the classroom. Think about the reading likes of the children in your classroom and what they would want to experience. Plan to include books that may reflect the interests of children as you have observed during play; for example, after noting student interest in digging to China, a teacher put out books on China and the Olympics. Try to display books that may be a part of the ongoing exploration and play in the classroom.

Include a variety of genres that appeal to growing minds, for example, interactive books, such as pop-ups for children to explore as well as informational books with large pictures and organizational maps. Although many teachers and parents believe that children are more interested in stories than informational books, an explosion of nonfiction picture books in recent years attests to children's insatiable demand for books about things that interest them. Picture books, such as I Spy, ask children to develop their visual literacy skills.

As part of providing texts that interest children, choose books that are culturally relevant to the children in your group. Books should offer positive messages about different cultures and viewpoints. Care should be taken to screen out books that offer broadly stereotypical or offensive depictions of any ethnic group, either in the stories or their illustrations. The collection should be multicultural, with titles representing the literature and characters of varied ethnic and cultural groups.

Choosing Culturally Relevant Books

Consider these questions when choosing texts intended to interest your students:

- Does the story foster the idea that we should value different cultures, linguistic backgrounds, religions, genders, and social classes?
- Do you have dual language texts that celebrate students' home languages?
- Does the story relate to the home literacy practices of your students?
- Do gender roles avoid stereotypical representations?
- Are ethnic minority characters shown in positions of power?
- Are any illustrations appropriately sized?
- Does the book have an easy-to-follow story line?
- Does the book give insight into how people live their lives, paying attention to culture and experiences?
- Is the language appropriate and does it have repetition?
- Does the story engage the reader through interaction, such as by opening flaps?

Books should also show some gender balance. Boys, for example, will often gravitate towards action-oriented stories, stories that feature a mischievous protagonist, or basic nonfiction. Girls sometimes have quite separate interests. A balance in the depiction of roles assumed by story characters of each gender should be sought. Given space and budget, try to balance these objectives out.

Creating a reading space

Here are some guidelines for creating a reading space:

- If possible, choose a corner — it is likely ideal.
- Place books flat and facing out so children are able to see and read the covers.
- Hold books in containers according to the genre.
- Create inviting seating with pillows, beanbag chairs, and carpet squares, or mats with children's names on them.
- Display books of early reader interest — ABC and 123 concept books, wordless picture books, predictable books (with repetitive text or text that closely matches pictures), informational picture books, and early reader books.
- Choose books that represent a variety of genres. Look at traditional literature, such as fairy tales, folktales, and nursery rhymes; nonfiction; songbooks; and realistic fiction.
- Provide storytelling props — a special blanket, puppets, flannel boards with cutouts of book characters, puppets, dress-up clothes, shakers, and musical instruments.
- Make available a tape player with headphones and audiobooks.
- Provide CD-ROM interactive storyboards, if you have a computer available.

The Writing Centre

In addition to providing a good Book Centre, teachers should include space and materials for children to experiment with writing. One way to do this is to provide a Writing Centre at which children can play with writing. The youngest children often "write" using broad scribbles, which befit their level of fine motor development and their definition of writing. For many young children, writing is defined as putting marks on paper (or any other appealing surface). Their scribbles are similar to an infant's babbling. Just as an infant babbles to experiment with the sounds he or she can make, taking pleasure in repetition as well as variety, so do novice writers delight in discovering the infinite combination of marks that they can make; they find satisfaction in gaining sufficient control to deliberately repeat the same marks. Thus, for the youngest children, writing takes on characteristics of both exploratory and practice play.

A good writing area encourages this playful exploration and practice. Here are key characteristics:

- A display of the alphabet is especially helpful to those children who are ready to experiment with conventional print, moving from letter-like forms to real letters, using either invented or conventional spelling.
- Children will also experiment with the alphabet if stamps or stencils of letters are provided.
- Many children enjoy manipulating magnetic letters on small magnetic boards; after forming words that interest them, some children try to copy their words onto paper to preserve them.

Children at this age will likely seek out centre materials that facilitate the writing they want to produce in support of their exploration of themes and their project work. Beyond their exploratory and practice play at a Writing Centre, preschool and Kindergarten students will immerse themselves in construction: creating a piece of writing that will serve a specific and personal purpose.

> "Play nourishes every aspect of a child's development — physical, social, emotional, intellectual, and creative. The learning in play is integrated, powerful, and largely invisible to the untrained eye."
> — Dr. Jane Hewes

Book Making as a Way of Writing

Making books is a fascinating activity for children from Kindergarten through the early grades. There are many different approaches to making them, depending on what skill level the children have achieved and what areas the class is studying.

The simplest way to make a book involves nothing more than a sheet of paper folded into four and then cut into four smaller pieces along the fold. Stapled together, they form a book of four pages. Two such pieces of paper will yield eight pages. Most children will enjoy the assembly and cutting as much as the drawing and printing.

The subjects need not be complex. Here are a few suggestions, but the idea lends itself to just about anything.

- *Number Books:* Each book focuses on one assigned number. The student either draws or procures images to represent that number or count that quantity of objects.
- *Alphabet Books:* These work with letters of the alphabet. The child either draws something that begins with the letter or seeks out images and prints representations of the letter.
- *I Can Books:* The first page starts with the phrase "I can . . ." All subsequent pages contain images of activities the child is able to perform.
- *I Would Like Books:* Similarly, the first page states, "I would like . . ." Subsequent pages illustrate activities that the child would like to be able to do.

Children also enjoy deconstructing the form of the book. Concertina books are interesting — they are made by folding a piece of paper repeatedly until it forms an accordion shape. These sorts of books can be illustrated by a continuous picture, perhaps one done by different children. Another interesting book form is the strip book. A strip book consists of pages that are divided horizontally, so that the viewed page can be one combined from strips of a different page. These can be used to combine pictures or short sentences in different and surprising ways.

Here are some criteria for creating a Writing Centre:

- Choose a quiet space away from other centres.
- Provide a round table for discussions and conferences.
- Make available pencils, pens, washable markers (thick and fine point), pencil crayons, pencil leads, crayons, chalk, glitter glue, and sparkles.
- Display an alphabet strip at each seat.
- Make available letter stamps.
- Set out magnetic letters.
- Post a list of theme-related words or create a related word wall.
- Display books related to class themes and projects.
- Make available letter and rhyming games.
- Provide paper of various sizes, colors, textures, and functions.

The Blocks Centre

"I like to build tall tall stuff so it don't fall down."
— Child (age 4)

"I like it when we just play at the centres. We work hard to make stuff. We pretend that we are builders and stuff."
— Child (age 6)

At the Blocks Centre, there should be enough unit blocks for children to build large constructions such as the walls of a castle. A smooth rug is a desirable feature for play. It is also helpful to provide vehicles such as toy cars, trucks, airplanes, tractors, and fire engines.

As far as promoting reading and writing at the centre goes, aim to provide the following resources:

- traffic and road signs
- plans, such as blueprints for construction
- pencils, markers, graph paper, and paper to produce signs for constructions
- labels for types of constructions, such as bridge, tower, castle, and house
- books on architecture

Play as Scaffolding for Literacy Success

Children benefit from a combination of explicit instruction and opportunities to play. They learn best when they can use their language and literacy skills to interact with the world and with one another — achieving this requires a degree of explicit instruction. It is just as important that time and space be made to allow children to play with language, with print, with words, letters, and sounds. As we have seen, they can do this in the structured space of a classroom literacy or role-playing centre, or at home during casual conversation. Society places a premium on good reading and writing skills, with both achieved as early and as fluently as possible.

The environment is a vital part of furthering this process. From children's earliest steps with oral language and sounds, to their first attempts to draw letters, creating an environment that encourages playful exploration of language is simple, but important. A print-rich environment does not require expensive technology or computer toys, just a healthy and thoughtful approach on the part of educators and parents.

Either way, whatever direction we as adults give to the play, we must remember that it has to reflect children's vision and interests, and work towards their emergent understandings of language and how it works. Time must be made to allow children to progress through the various developmental stages. All children learn at a different pace, and culture, gender, class, and the other perceptions and interests they bring to school must all be taken into account. Play allows them to gain confidence and skills in a fun and engaging way, a way that reinforces and scaffolds learning without their being aware of it. Guided play also allows the teacher to gear lessons and learning to all children.

Finally, we must remember that to children, playing is their work. If the adults in their lives use play as part of their learning, and are eager and willing to participate, then the children will also see learning as part of their social and community worlds. Language and literacy are achieved not by the use of a strict hierarchy of lesson plans, but by a steady immersion in a rich environment, where the children's explorations are constantly rewarded with new knowledge.

More than once we have used the term *scaffolding*. In this context, scaffolding is how educators create tasks that provide a knowledge base for later, more complex achievements. Using play creatively to encourage emergent literacy is all about scaffolding. Whether discussing alphabet sounds with a young child or providing a Writing Centre, our goal should be to use children's own natural inclinations for play to create a base for future literacy and language success.

4

Play as a Path to Problem Solving: Mathematics

When we talk about introducing young children to math, it is more than the nuts and bolts of arithmetic that we are referring to. Beyond simple addition and subtraction, numeracy is the ability to reason with and understand mathematical concepts as applicable to our lived lives. For young children, math encompasses a whole world of problem solving, the development of logical thinking, the verbalizing of numbers, and the ways and means by which they can quantify and categorize their world. Math also offers an enormous repository of games and other play-based opportunities for learning and skill building. From the daily routines of both classroom and home — the calendar, snack time, routine lineup, and more — there abound playful opportunities to put problem-solving skills to practical use.

Numeracy, which is to numbers what literacy is to text, is the natural outcome of these scaffolding exercises. Estimation, patterning, observation, seriation, and number recognition are part of children's everyday lives, and we can find numerous possibilities for playful exploration.

Math Concepts and the Young Child

"I play jumping with my friends. We like to sing and jump and count . . ."
— Child (age 6)

Almost from the moment children are aware of the world around them, they are starting to learn math concepts. Every day they have experiences that encourage their numeracy. Sorting by size, color, or shape is an early learning skill — stacking blocks and cups are even found in the playpen. Preschool activities such as sharing snacks and passing out toys develop concepts of counting and seriation. How many parents count stairs while leading a child up and down, or count the number of red cars on a family trip? Either is a subtle yet ubiquitous playful counting exercise. As soon as children can articulate "yes" and "no," "one more" is likely to join their personal phrasebooks.

Research has revealed that ". . . children, even preschoolers, have surprisingly powerful everyday (informal) arithmetic knowledge" (Baroody & Dowker, 2003, p. 750). Further to this, other researchers, including Griffiths (2005), have supported the necessity of introducing mathematical concepts as early as possible. The earlier the foundation is laid, the stronger the problem-solving skills for later success.

As is the case with print literacy, children need to become comfortable with mathematics and math concepts in the world of numbers and order before they can work with them in earnest. A pile of classroom worksheets, suddenly descending on them in Grade 1, is not the best way to create this comfort. Numeracy must be part of the every day, part of their lived lives and play, part of the creative experience that is playful learning. When children see math concepts as part of their world and important to meaning making within that world, then they will gain confidence in numbers and how they can express them; this, in turn, will help build a strong mathematical foundation.

Math Conversations in the Home

Before you, as an educator, can communicate with children about math, they must understand what you are talking about. While this may seem self-evident, achieving it can be trickier than one might think. Beyond fairly explicit instruction on the part of both teachers and parents, it involves using mathematical language in a normal, everyday fashion to create a solid base of math awareness for the child.

When talking with parents, offer suggestions on where and how to build awareness of math concepts.

- At home, for example, bath time offers a great chance for application-based instruction. Children love to play with water. A set of measuring cups will provide an easy way to demonstrate the difference in measurement between a half cup and a full cup.
- Setting the table with forks and spoons allows a child to use one-to-one correspondence.
- Putting toys away can be made into a game of addition and subtraction.
- Even something as simple as sharing a snack can be made into a game and an opportunity for the child to talk about numbers. For example, the adult can ask the child to give out four carrot sticks and keep five, then ask for two more . . .

Shapes, which are easily found in the home and early-grade classroom, are the basis of geometry. Street signs, for example, offer a great opportunity for guessing games: "See that sign up ahead? Is that a triangle or a rectangle?" Shapes are all around us, and when you begin to notice them, you can also call a child's attention to them. It is important that the child realizes a shape does not exist only on a page — using the environment is a good way to help that concept along.

While graphing is probably more of a classroom activity, at its simplest, it can be a great way to establish higher mathematical language concepts, such as "more than" or "equal." This is especially true when the graphing activity is shared.

In Cecile's Grade 1 class, the children have been working on the math concept of measurement. They are asked to estimate and measure using common classroom objects. Cecile first invites the children to make hypotheses, posing questions such as "About how many of these pencils are equal in weight to these wooden blocks?" She asks students to choose three classroom objects to measure mass. After they provide an estimate of what each object would weigh, the children gather around the set of scales in the classroom to weigh the objects on their own. They then graph the objects from lightest to heaviest, showing how some objects weigh more than others or may be equal in mass. During this exploration, Cecile still poses questions: "Would three pencils necessarily weigh the same as three blocks?" "Would 25 paper clips definitely weigh more than one block?"

When children are talking and playing together, they become much more comfortable with the language concepts. Being able to "try things out" is the sign of a safe environment. The implicit instruction provided by their mutual explorations is just as likely to have a lasting effect as a similar way of explicit instruction.

Most children are generally intrigued and excited by mastering simple mathematical concepts, and are motivated to do well. Quantifying their world is one of the great games of childhood. By providing them with the means to do it, we help lay the foundation upon which much more complex knowledge will be built.

Books on Math Concepts

Picture books that illustrate mathematical concepts stimulate language development and interaction with text. Several recommended titles are listed below.

- *Mouse Numbers & Letters* by Jim Arnosky
- *Don't Count Your Chicks* by Ingri D'Aulaire and Edgar D'Aulaire
- *Adding Animals* by Colin Hawkins
- *The Doorbell Rang* by Pat Hutchins
- *Inch by Inch: The Garden Song* by David Mallett
- *How Many Seeds in a Pumpkin?* by Margaret McNamara
- *Off and Counting* by Sally Noll
- *Animal Patterns* by Nathan Olson
- *Shapes* by John J. Reiss
- *There Was an Old Lady Who Swallowed a Fly* by Simms Taback

---

Bridging Home and School with Positive Math Language

In the earliest stages of children's schooling, parents need to be intimately involved with building a foundation of mathematical numeracy. There are a couple of key components of this scaffolding and bridging process. It may be helpful to explain to parents how children learn, using ideas presented below.

Teaching mathematics — A constructivist vision

- Knowledge is created in children by interactions with the environment and their community.
- Children go through many stages as they build their knowledge, from basic concrete understandings to more abstract thinking.
- School uses a developmental instructional approach, where children are constantly building on previous experiences.
- Children's thinking is engaged by the discovery of patterns and relationships between numbers and their world.
- Children should learn to communicate their growing understanding of numeracy in both verbal and written fashions.

Parents should understand that their involvement is vital for their child's future problem-solving abilities. Most parents will already know that students with engaged parents do better, but it is useful to reinforce that their active participation will help strengthen the knowledge base upon which children's later learning will be raised.

First, however, the teacher may have to combat some of the parents' own misconceptions and prejudices about math instruction. Math instruction may be very different from when the parents attended school. Many parents will recall with dismay their own math experiences and will be nervous about taking an active role in their children's education. It may be helpful to remember these common math misconceptions — likely all too common among parents:

- Math is just about sums, times tables, and other exercises.
- The only way to learn math is by repetitive worksheets.
- Only some people are good at math — boys are better at it than girls.
- You need to be a teacher to understand math.
- Math is the hardest core subject.

The line master on the next page outlines some concrete ways parents can aid their children in mathematical learning.

Building Numeracy in Kindergarten

Building numeracy in the early grades utilizes a great resource, namely, children's natural curiosity about the world and their need to quantify it in logical and sensible terms. To some degree, if children are given the right tools, numeracy will be intuitive. In order to take advantage of this natural tendency and need for order in a child's worldview, we have to provide games and activities that are within their developmental capacity and that they can use and understand.

In Kindergarten, good teachers introduce math concepts gradually, using hands-on centres and active problem solving, keeping the explorations as tangible and tactile as possible. As a rule of thumb, early numeracy in Kindergarten can be divided into four distinct areas:

1. *Number Sense:* The first stage of numeracy, number sense refers to establishing what counting is, as well as ordering, comparing, and establishing the relationship between the printed symbol of a number and the quantity it represents.
2. *Patterns:* Children recognize the patterns in the world around them and begin to use numbers to quantify them. Ideally, they will use this knowledge to begin predicting the solutions to problems and what happens next in a given pattern.
3. *Measurement:* Children learn to compare objects on the basis of length, capacity, mass, or amount. Part and parcel of this is the ability to describe measurements and the differences between various measures.
4. *Numeracy Development:* This means the ability to put all of the above aspects together. Children should solve problems on their own, show an understanding of cause and effect, identify similarities and differences between things in their environment, and demonstrate a clear understanding about the links between printed numbers and actual amounts.

Good Kindergarten curriculum planning includes all of the above areas with everything building towards numeracy development. When planning lessons and classroom activities and games, teachers will find it helpful to adopt the following guidelines:

How to Help Your Children Do Math

- First, become involved in your children's learning. Since all teachers are interested in extending children's school knowledge to the home, don't hesitate to ask questions, perhaps for an example to illustrate a mathematical concept. Be sure to understand what the curriculum goals are, and keep abreast of classroom activities. Doing so will help you feel like much more than a homework supervisor.

- Children need to see that math can be both interesting and fun. Small games, such as Snakes and Ladders, Bingo, I Spy, and Pick-up Sticks, everyday questions, and helping-out-around-the-house activities can all promote math learning and also provide great opportunities to make it fun.

- Numeracy is the ability to express mathematical concepts and mathematical reasoning. It involves applying numerical symbols in ways that help us quantify our world and experiences. Model numeracy, drawing on aspects of your environment. Children need to see you use math in a practical sense: "Let's see. There are five people eating supper tonight. How many forks, spoons, and knives do we need?"

- Share opportunities to meet mathematical objectives with your children: "How many houses are between us and the Stop sign? Let's count."

- Counting or 1-2-3 books can help children gain an understanding of numbers. They can learn to count the number of objects on a page and group according to characteristics (e.g., size and color). Find examples from your family life to help children connect to the learning from the book.

- Make use of nursery rhymes and poems. Many of these use numbers, as in "One, two, buckle my shoe" or "Five little ducks went swimming one day."

- Choose magazines that feature brightly colored pictures to encourage counting and the basics of addition and subtraction.

- Make math a part of your everyday chores — the idea is to develop mathematical ideas through language. As you or your child tidy up, count the items. Use the toys in the toy box in a number of ways, perhaps asking, "How many pieces of puzzle are you holding? How many do I have in my hand? Let's see how many blue toys are in the toy box. Which toy is closest to the television? the door? How do you know? Can you show me how?"

- Use language to develop children's mathematical concepts about counting and comparing. Examples: how many, more or less, greater or smaller, longer or shorter, higher or lower, and heavier or lighter.

- You can also encourage understanding of direction and position. Work such phrases as these into your conversation: in front or behind, up and down, top or bottom, next to or beside, before or after, inside or outside, over, under, and below.

- Keep any negative attitudes about mathematics to yourself — children are very sensitive to the ideas of their parents. Be positive and so will they.

Planning guidelines

- Ask questions that are open-ended and encourage mathematical thinking.
- Use games that encourage cooperation and require the children to talk to one another to find solutions — oral language is very important.
- Integrate mathematical and numeracy language into other learning areas such as science and social studies and activities.
- Use activities and games that offer more than one solution to a problem and require some degree of critical thinking. For example, the measurement activities in Cecile's classroom, described above, called for critical thinking.
- Incorporate gross motor activities with math. Getting children up and moving facilitates learning concepts such as addition and subtraction, as well as shapes. It also makes math fun! Have children group themselves using their bodies according to numbers: "Form a group of five and make a triangle." "What if we need to show the four corners of a square? How many people do we need?"
- Give children opportunity to talk about their experiences and discoveries through a sharing time. Ask children to describe the types of activities they did on the weekend. If they went shopping at the market, they could talk about the amount and types of foods purchased; if they took a drive to the cottage, they could talk about the shapes seen along the way. There are many ways to have children talk about how numeracy defines their everyday lives.

Playful Approaches to Numeracy at Home and School

"Sometimes people forget that play is learning and learning is play."
— Peter Dixon

A play-based approach will help children relate numbers, measurement, patterns, and equations to their environment. During the early years, the adult will lead the play to a higher degree, asking questions and demonstrating the scenarios. As the children get older and their numeracy grows, they will begin to take charge of the play, and cooperate and communicate more about the problem solving. The key to developing numeracy is asking questions that will get the children thinking.

To make this section more accessible, I have divided it into three sections: play-based activities (1) for the home, where the foundation for numeracy begins; (2) for the late preschool and Kindergarten; and (3) for the early grades. Together, these sections cover the emergent literacy phase.

Play-based activities for the home

Teachers cannot, of course, control what sorts of activities parents and their children engage in at home; however, the next page provides an outline of what parents could do to set the foundations of numeracy and promote it in the early years at home. It is presented in line master format so that you have the option to share it with school families.

Home Foundations for Numeracy

The key to building a numeracy foundation at home is to make math and numbers part of the everyday routine of chores, play, meals, and other household activities. You needn't turn your house into a quiz corner, but you can take advantage of the numeracy already part of your family's life and make a moderate effort to bring your children into it.

Getting Dressed: Ask young children to count everything they will be putting on. Play a timing game, counting the seconds as they get dressed. When they are putting clothes away, ask them to make patterns of socks and other garments in a drawer.

Measuring Height: Make a height chart, perhaps on a door, and get the children to measure themselves against it once a month.

Meal Time: Ask questions like "How many spoons are on the table?" Ask for help setting a table. "There are four of us eating. Can you find a fork for each of us?" Reverse the questions to encourage the child to think: "How many of us will eat tonight? How many glasses should I put out?"

Snack Time: Count snacks: "I think you have three carrots left. Is that right?" For the picky eater, you could divide a piece of hard fruit, perhaps an apple, into different shapes: "Can you eat a round piece now? How about a piece shaped like a triangle?"

Around the Home: Children at this age will probably not understand a real clock, but digital clocks allow you to show the use of numbers in a home. Many children enjoy simple counting games involving household geography: "How many steps to the washroom?" "Let's count the stairs while we walk down them." Sorting out cupboards and drawers, a lot of fun for many children, can provide a good opportunity to play with measurement and patterns. Ask the children to put the pots in a row, from biggest to smallest. Perhaps they could figure out which pot would make the most soup. Have the children use a ruler to measure household objects: "What's the tallest thing in the house? How wide is the door? Whose shoes are bigger — Mom's or Dad's'?"

Play Time: You don't need expensive technology to make numeracy-enhancing games part of a child's playtime. Matching games using simple cards, either store bought or hand made, fascinate some children and provide a great example of patterning and prediction. Stacking cups are cheap and easy to find, and for the very young child will provide great patterning and comparison games. Numbered blocks will do the same; for example, ask the child to make a tower of three or four blocks, starting at one and going up. If your child has a playmate, ask them to play a guessing game: "How many beads do I have in this box?" Hide and Seek requires counting, as do simple board games. Crafting will be a good activity for play-based numeracy — Popsicle sticks and pipe cleaners can be made into many things, but also can be counted, compared, and categorized. While coloring might not hold children's attention, sorting crayons by size or color might.

Bath Time: For many children, bath time is the highlight of their day, a chance to have the undivided attention of an adult and also play around with soap and water. A few cheap plastic cups of different sizes will create many opportunities to explore measurement.

Singing: All children love to sing, whether with a parent or other children. Many songs can be adapted to include a numeracy component or turned into a counting game. Familiar songs, like *This Old Man* and *Old MacDonald*, are ready examples, but a simple Internet search will provide many more.

Outside the Home: Shapes can be sought and discussed on a walk or drive: "What shape is that sign?" "Do you see anything round right now?" Counting can also be part of a walk: "How many steps is it to the sidewalk?" The park will provide a good place to play: "Let's pick up five pine cones — which one is the smallest? Which one is in the middle?" "Who is swinging higher — you or me?" "Let's hop to the slide. Who can hop the most? Let's count."

Play-based activities for late preschool and Kindergarten

Activities in late preschool and Kindergarten will allow great scope for exploring mathematics. Children are a little older and more sophisticated; more important, perhaps, they are now in a social environment. This environment allows interaction and cooperation, and other opportunities for the children to talk about and explore their numeracy together.

While the Internet and teacher guides offer thousands of worksheet possibilities, here are several activities that involve the children in a more hands-on process:

Pasta Sorting: Either as individuals or as teams, play a sorting game featuring different kinds of pasta. Give each child or group a selection of different pasta shapes, and then have them sort them by shape, size, or type. Similar games can be played with beads or counting chips.

Math Bingo: Create a simple bingo game for younger children. Give each child a card with about 20 numbers on it, from 1 to 10. Spin a wheel or turn up cards, and call out the numbers. As you do so, the students cross out the appropriate numbers on their cards. The first student to cross out all of them shouts, "Bingo!"

Class Matching: Play a game of matching cards, but do it on a large scale. Each child in a group holds a card with a shape on it, and either turns it upside down or keeps the shape hidden. Elsewhere in the class is another child with a matching card. A third child (or group) has to match the children and shapes by asking questions about the shapes without using shape names: "Is your shape like a box?" "Can your shape be used as a baseball diamond?" "Is your box like my eraser?" "Is your shape round?" "Does your shape look like a winter tree?"

Tic-Tac-Toe: This game can be made into a group activity by simply drawing the game on the board and dividing the children into small teams that have to decide on their move together — a good game for patterns and logic.

Simon Says (With a Math Twist): Like many other simple children's games, Simon Says can easily be given a mathematical slant: "Simon says touch your knees together three times. . . ."

Singing Games: As at home, nursery rhymes and other children's songs are well suited to numeracy. "Baa, baa, black sheep, have you any wool? Yes sir, yes sir, 10 bags full, . . . 9 bags full . . ." And so on.

Number Tag: Each child gets a sheet or card with a number on it from 1 to 10. One child, designated It, stands in a corner unable to see the rest of the children. The child calls out numbers from 1 to 10. Each time a number is chosen, all the children with that number sit down. Eventually, one child should be left — that person then becomes It.

Red Rover, Come Over: Play the old-fashioned game, but give it a numeric slant. Each child is assigned a number between 1 and 10. The caller stands opposite the children and says something like, "Red Rover, Red Rover, number seven come over!" Any child who has been given the number seven tries to cross the floor without being caught by the caller through a tap on the shoulder. The game continues with the calling of numbers until all children have been captured by the caller.

What Time Is It, Mr. Wolf?: Children line up at the back of the gym. When they ask, "What time is it, Mr. Wolf?" the wolf responds with a time, such as 10 a.m. The children must take 10 steps towards the wolf. After repeating the question-and-answer pattern three or four times, the wolf yells, "Supper time!" The students race to the back of the gym to avoid getting eaten. Children love to play this game.

The following games enhance understanding of mathematical concepts.

- *Guess the Number* —A teacher or a student chooses a number that others have to guess, the catch being that the number chooser has to provide a helpful clue: "My number is two plus four . . ."
- *Finish the Pattern* — Create a classroom maze using desks and chairs. A group of children needs to solve simple problems to progress.
- *The Estimation Container* — In this simple but intriguing game, children estimate how many objects are in a container. The game can work with either groups or individuals.

Morning Routine: Even activities such as the daily calendar and the days of the week can focus on numeracy. For instance, the children can count how many days are remaining until a special event or holiday. Students can also become aware of how many days they spend in school versus how many days they spend at home.

Math with Jelly Beans: Give each child a handful of various colored jelly beans and ask math questions. For example: "How many yellow and red jelly beans do you have?" If they wish, children can then eat the jelly beans as a special "math" treat!

Play-based activities for the early grades

By Grades 1 and 2, students are beginning to have a much firmer grasp on numeracy, which will allow the teacher to plan more elaborate games that require greater logical and reasoning skills, or a higher degree of collaboration.

The Lemonade Stand: This game requires some props, including cups and fake money, and would work well in a dramatic play centre. Essentially, two or three students run a lemonade stand. Their prices are fixed, but each customer places a different order. The stand holders have to figure out how much money they need to charge or how much change to give back. This activity can be made as elaborate as desired, depending on the students' ages and capabilities.

Silent Order: In this game for Grade 1 students, the teacher assigns each student a number between 1 and 15 or 20. The students then have to line up, in order, starting at 1 and doing it in silence. If the game is too easy for older or more advanced students, assign the numbers by twos, or have students line up in reverse order.

Measure the Class: This is the home rainy-day game with an amusing twist. Instead of a ruler, use paper clips. A child lies on the floor while other students use many paper clips to measure the child. The average first or second grader will enjoy the counting (and recounting) of the paper clips to determine the child's length.

Class Fractions: Create three groups of students: one with four students, one with six, and one with eight; then, ask other children fractional questions: "How many children in the second group have to move if one-third of them need to sit down?" The result will be some confusion but also a memorable lesson for the children, who will likely be amused as their peers become equations.

Measurement Scavenger Hunt: When children get more comfortable with measurement, stage a class scavenger hunt; for example, ask children to find objects that are at least 5 cm long or weigh at least 500 g.

Board Games: Older children who can understand rules will enjoy straightforward board games like Trouble, Snakes and Ladders, and possibly Monopoly. These games require significant counting skills, as well as basic addition and subtraction.

Guessing Circumference: Circumference can be a hard geometrical principle to explain. Getting the class to estimate and then measure the circumferences of objects like a globe, soccer ball, hockey puck, or drink container will make for an illuminating and memorable exercise.

Cards: Simple card games, such as War, Old Maid, and Crazy Eights, teach children how to recognize numbers, as well as logical sequencing.

Count on Spelling: This newer game combines both literacy and numeracy. Children have a limited time to guess the numeric value of a word — to count the letters and then add them up. In other words, "classroom" equals 9; "books" equals 5. This game is good as an oral exercise; the teacher reads the word, and the class then has to figure out the numeric value without seeing the word written down.

Poll Voting on the Class Pet's Name: Involve the class in voting on the name of a class pet or stuffed animal. Each child is allowed to vote only once using a simple piece of paper and placing the ballot in a shoebox. Count up the votes and list all of the suggested names; the class then selects the top three names and the final vote takes place. After the voting is over, have the class draw a bar graph to show the results of the final vote.

The Role of a Math Centre

A Math Centre encourages children's physical manipulation of objects and learning through exploration and discovery. It is full of materials that will foster mathematical thinking (see diagram on the next page). The materials, which will vary with children's ages and experiences, allow children to playfully explore mathematical thinking processes, such as sorting, classifying, comparing, patterning, and measuring. A Math Centre is meant to promote playful exploration just as much as a Writing or Book Centre does.

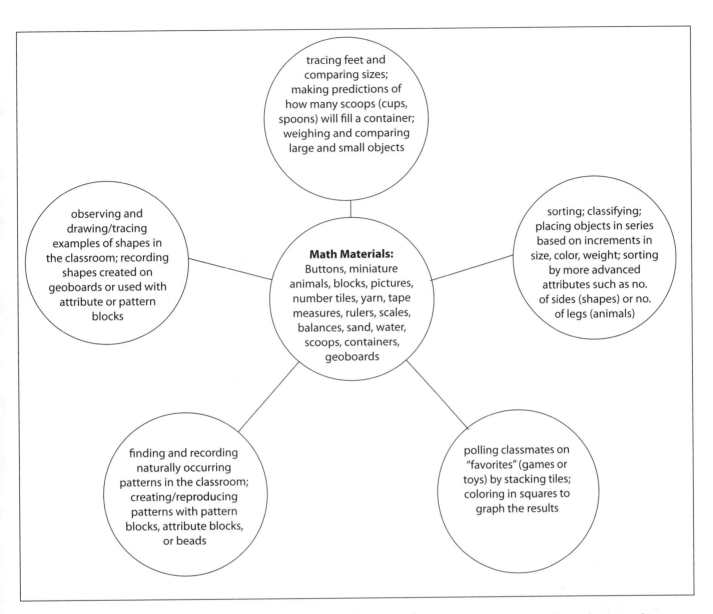

Math Materials:
Buttons, miniature animals, blocks, pictures, number tiles, yarn, tape measures, rulers, scales, balances, sand, water, scoops, containers, geoboards

tracing feet and comparing sizes; making predictions of how many scoops (cups, spoons) will fill a container; weighing and comparing large and small objects

sorting; classifying; placing objects in series based on increments in size, color, weight; sorting by more advanced attributes such as no. of sides (shapes) or no. of legs (animals)

observing and drawing/tracing examples of shapes in the classroom; recording shapes created on geoboards or used with attribute or pattern blocks

finding and recording naturally occurring patterns in the classroom; creating/reproducing patterns with pattern blocks, attribute blocks, or beads

polling classmates on "favorites" (games or toys) by stacking tiles; coloring in squares to graph the results

Children need a hands-on approach in order to build mathematical reasoning and critical understanding of how mathematics is very much a part of their everyday life — they do not come to understand numbers naturally. As teachers, we must provide activities that illustrate various understandings about math, keeping in mind that the relationships between these ideas are often abstract. Successful numeracy programs require children to see numbers, counting, and measurement in the contexts of their lives.

When discussing new and familiar tasks with students, it is important to help them make life connections to mathematical reasoning — doing so will give them power over their own learning (Baroody & Dowker, 2003). As Lev Vygotsky argued, teachers need to provide scaffolding for children's discoveries from exploring, reasoning, and resolving problems through interactive play-based activities. When exploring numeracy, children should always feel safe and valued and believe that their ideas count. Having time for play and exploration helps children see how mathematics is connected to their real lives and appreciate the value of the mathematical concepts. The use of manipulatives and games, as discussed in this chapter, enhances the learning styles of many children. Above all, learning mathematics must be an active exploration to enhance numeracy.

5

Play as a Form of Exploration: Science

One of the most satisfying and successful ways to use play as an educational platform is through the exploration of science. By its very nature, science is hands-on and enhances curiosity in children. With just the most subtle direction, children can come to learn, and prepare to learn, in a wide variety of ways. And they can do so while playing in ways they find highly interesting.

Scientific reasoning includes a number of key learning experiences, experiences that can be a part of either guided or free play (Howe & Davies, 2005). While some of these experiences are more important than others at various stages, all are inherently part of the most basic scientific explorations.

The skills and experiences that children can absorb from scientific play range from the basic to the complex. They include the following:

- predicting
- recognizing the importance of curiosity about the world
- problem-solving
- showing environmental sensitivity and responsibility
- charting and writing down information and findings
- becoming aware of life and life cycles
- demonstrating logic and a sense of cause and effect

Discovery through Play

"Children learn as they play. Most importantly, in play children learn how to learn."
— O. Fred Donaldson

Children's play that deliberately includes scientific experimentation and exploration will reflect and develop its goals from the experiences listed above. A love of discovery as an end in itself should be the ultimate goal of the play. While other concrete goals, such as record keeping, validating ideas, and recognizing logical processes are invaluable, they are really secondary outcomes. In essence, we are trying to open children's minds to possibilities. Especially in younger children, encouraging the idea that the world can be explained, changed, or just marveled at may be enough.

We can, of course, narrow that rather lofty goal into a few key areas: exploration, discovery, creativity, and problem solving.

For the children, scientific *exploration* is a science-oriented activity in which an outcome is not easily predicted. While it is possible that a prediction about the outcome can be made, it is not one readily obvious to the child. The absence of specific outcomes or tasks is the key aspect of exploration. Such activities encourage the child to be open-minded, with freedom to discover how any number of things and processes might work.

During scientific play that involves *discovery*, children acquire specific knowledge and understanding. Not every episode of scientific play has to lead to a discovery. That said, it can be a powerful motive towards more detailed and elaborate activities.

Creativity should be found in almost any kind of scientific play. When provided with the right tools and circumstances, children will be able to see events from changing perspectives, make surprising connections, or alter their previous understandings. They should be able to alter the play so that they can reach their own conclusions or alter events to create their own outcomes. Either way, fostering an open-minded approach to science and to life in general can be a positive outcome of such play.

Finally, by its nature, scientific play produces and enhances *problem-solving* skills. Children learn to identify a problem, figure out what question they are trying to answer, discover ways to go about answering it, try various solutions, and then decide which one worked the best — or the worst. These skills also involve critical and original thinking, as well as the other three skills discussed above. While problem solving is crucial to science, it is also valuable in most other aspects of a child's growing mind. If children can discover ways to answer their own scientific questions, they are well on the way to becoming first-rate creative thinkers; they are also likely to gain enhanced self-esteem and a general enthusiasm about the educational process.

In the reflection below, Kindergarten teacher Susan Barron describes how two of her young students tried out a few different possible solutions to a problem that concerned them.

Wanted — A Lost Frog: Problem Solving

I observed two little girls who were searching for a little toy frog known as Froggy that had become misplaced somewhere in the classroom. The girls were very worried about the toy frog and began to ask their friends questions to see if they could discover his whereabouts. This strategy proved unsuccessful, so they decided to make up little posters with Froggy's picture on them to pass out to their classmates, in hopes that seeing a picture would jog their memories and Froggy would be returned. The pictures they drew were quite detailed, but again, they were not able to bring their friend back safely.

I remember thinking to myself that this is great imaginative play, which demonstrated genuine effort to use the new skills they had. They are talking and listening to each other, and are writing and drawing things (like maps and posters), which have a real purpose and meaning for them.

— Susan Barron

Subtle differences between very young children and their elders should be kept in mind when establishing goals for scientific play. In the earliest stages of their education, basic science helps children to begin connecting the dots between the elements of their worlds. Specific *how* and *why* questions are not really the point; instead, we try to help them realize that they can ask questions, solve problems, or begin to make connections between themselves and the world. Sensory information and personal explorations are invaluable. Older children, or at least those

"Creative play is like a spring that bubbles up from deep within a child."
— Joan Almon

who have developed more organized thought processes, can use more knowledge-based experiments. Chemical reactions, static electricity, and the surprising effects of physics are best left to them.

For any age, however, educators and parents should focus on a couple of basic principles. First, the activity should accomplish something. Activities that demonstrate why something *doesn't* happen are unlikely to fulfill any of the above criteria. Second, activities that in some way relate to the child's own observations of life and nature are more likely to have some lasting positive effect.

For very young children, these activities are not designed to fit any particular curriculum goal, other than stimulating their creativity and curiosity. For those in Kindergarten and the early grades, the activities can easily be routed towards more concrete goals. Even the simplest of experiments will enhance children's abilities in observation, classification, quantification, communication, and inference. All of these will not, and cannot, be present in every science play; however, over a term or a year all can be readily enhanced through enjoyable and interesting scientific activities.

How to Introduce Hands-on Science

So, having decided to introduce a scientific element into children's play, where does the educator start? Making use of a common-sense understanding of young children's learning styles will quickly eliminate many areas. For example, anything dangerous is out, as are activities that require a lengthy wait or a long list of successive ingredients. Young children are impatient and self-centred. While they often have expansive imaginations, they are not given to abstract thinking. Easily distracted, they are far more excited by doing something than by having it explained.

Educators, therefore, should be steered in their scientific approaches by the following guidelines:

- clear objectives
- simple, clear instructions
- hands-on experiences
- easily attainable results

Children at any age are interested in their own environment. Water is ubiquitous and easy to come by. It offers a host of scientific possibilities for any age group. Preschoolers may enjoy doing simple experiments demonstrating how water can be transformed into ice and then back into water. Kindergarten students can perform experiments that use water to play with concepts about mass and volume, say, how an object's material affects its flotation. Primary students may benefit from, and understand, more complex ideas, such as how water can be used as a force for movement, through something like a simple home-made water mill.

Whatever the topic, it is important to adopt the child's perspective. As soon as concepts become too complicated, the play will be abandoned. *Keeping it simple* has to be the watchword. And we must never forget the key element of any play experience: it has to be fun. If the play gets dull or obviously educational, the delight of scientific play will be lost.

Thematically, the more the scientific activity relates to other aspects of children's lives, the more it will likely resonate later on in their learning. Effective

"Young children are busy exploring and experimenting with the social world as well as the elements, plants and animals, the cosmos. In these explorations and through their questions, children are creating their own learning experiences. They are strengthening their ideas about sameness and difference, growth and change. These experiences are essential to the development of reasoning tools."

— David Elkind, *The Power of Play*

teachers already know that a few good themes, repeated regularly, work better than a huge number of ideas. For example, to use the water theme from above, in the winter the children could play with snow, which the teacher could relate to an indoor experience, like melting ice-cubes. In April, spring rains could be brought into a water-related environmental theme. In either case, experiments could be as simple as discovering how quickly snow melts or as complex as measuring the effect of rainfall and erosion. The key elements in the success of the play will be the educator's patience, the sensory experience of the play, and the way the play stimulates the child's natural curiosity and sense of discovery.

The Discovery Centre

Play scenarios based on scientific principles and discoveries need not rely on expensive equipment or technology. As most parents can testify, children are often as fascinated by a stack of blocks as they are by an expensive video game. Play scenarios depend on the imagination.

Many preschool and Kindergarten rooms incorporate what is known as a Discovery Centre. Best located near a window and a water source, it is a special space intended to encourage creative and discovery play. It should be big enough to allow at least a few children to cooperate or play in a parallel fashion, and sturdy enough that spills and messes are easily dealt with. Based around a large table set at a child's level, it could incorporate the following items:

- containers for water
- sand or soil, pebbles or gravel
- small plants or wooden sticks
- tools for measuring, like cups and spoons
- sturdy magnifying glasses
- string and fabric
- shells, pebbles, or small blocks
- small tools, like rakes and shovels
- magnets and small metal objects
- soaps
- feathers and small Styrofoam shapes
- cookie cutters
- sponges and colanders
- plastic tubes, small hoses, and straws
- food coloring

Of course, all materials need to be safe or big enough not to be swallowed. These materials can be changed regularly and should lend themselves to repeated or multiple use. Encourage children to recycle and to bring in useful household materials, like toilet-paper tubes and plastic bottles, for the centre.

Once the centre is set up, it will not take long for children to gravitate towards it. If all you have on hand is water and soil, the centre will already be irresistible to just about any child to whom getting wet is a passion. With a subtle hand, children can be easily pointed towards any number of scientific experiments. Any and all activities should involve a basic question that the child can answer independently through physical involvement in the play. While the centre serves as the base for such scientific experiences and experiments, these can also occur in other spaces.

Science Play: Types and Examples

Children's natural curiosity is an invaluable educational resource. While just about any scientific principle can be explored to one degree or another by children, here are some areas that particularly lend themselves to school and preschool classrooms.

Measurement play

Measurement activities can be interesting for the smallest children right up to those in their primary years. Children perform and repeat an activity in various fashions, ideally measuring the differing results. Small children can play with simple questions, older ones with more elaborate ones.

A common play scenario asks which container holds more of a given substance. Using containers of different sizes and shapes, or transferring water from one container to another will be fun and instructive for preschoolers. Older children might be intrigued by exploring concepts of displacement — for example, measuring how a heavy object causes more water to spill from a container than a bigger, lighter one. Comparing and contrasting various objects and their properties can be turned into a guessing game or one involving blindfolds for an amusing sensory experience.

Other measurement scenarios involve time and gravity (but keep the terminology to a minimum). Little boys love racing toy cars. A simple raceway made of cardboard tubes can be used to demonstrate concepts of weight and speed. Whose car goes faster? farther? Why? Time can be measured by making a chart about when the sun sets each day, a fascinating subject in more northern places.

Temperature offers a myriad of measurement possibilities. Sun and shade can be examined by leaving objects in a sunny window. The aforementioned ice-cube can prompt discovery in a number of ways: How fast does it melt? How much water is left over? Does the ice-cube feel the same to different parts of the body?

Physical science play

Many adults find physics to be a difficult and intimidating part of their education, but this need not be the case for the young child. Simple concepts can lead to productive play scenarios. Such play should focus primarily on movement and the relationships between moving objects. As children change their actions, they should be able to see a similar change in the object or the object's relations to others. Sounds complex, but the play itself can be straightforward, educational, and still lots of fun.

For example, twirling a basket of fabric around can teach children about centrifugal forces. The first time they do it, everything falls out. As they twirl the basket faster, everything stays in. Gravity can be explored by dropping objects: What falls faster — feathers or plastic toys? What rolls down a slope faster — a big ball or a small one? a heavy one or a light one? Such scenarios are limited only to the child's capacity for fun.

"Children learn so much through play. Outsiders might see children just playing in the sand or just playing with water, but the children are actually learning as they play. Amongst many things, they learn about textures, weights, measures, structures, what it means to share what they know and question what they don't know."
— Shawna Brooke, Kindergarten Teacher

"For young children, play and learning are inextricably linked, the one often leading from the other."
— Dr. Ann Langston and Dr. Leslie Abbott

Friction is a difficult concept to explain, but one that children grasp easily when they experiment with it. What moves faster along a floor — rubber sneakers or stocking feet? How can you make something more slippery or sticky? Pushing and pulling are usually a source of parental and educator frustration, but they can be turned into a useful experiment, too. How many children do you need to pull a slippery object? What about a rough or heavy one?

Water is particularly useful for demonstrating physical properties in a playful fashion. Older children can build small pendulums or maybe water wheels from simple craft supplies. Filling an old coffee can with water and then getting children to punch a few holes in the plastic cover will provide them with a good demonstration of water pressure. Sponges allow them to explore principles of absorption. Soap bubbles are an endless source of fascination.

Biology play

Children are fascinated by the workings of their own bodies. Such scenarios can be based around the Discovery Centre or take place elsewhere in the play space.

While such issues need to be handled sensitively, differences in hair color, height, shoe size, and so on can be measured and compared (see image below). Hands and feet can be traced and then compared every month. Cheap magnifying glasses can be used to examine skin or other natural objects. At snack time, children can compare how different food tastes or feels in their mouths. Ask them to plug their noses while they taste their favorite foods — do they still taste them? Even clean-up time offers opportunities to explore questions: Why does soap help clean dirty hands? What makes our hands dirtier — sand, soil, or flour?

As part of an exploration of how to sort themselves, a class graph shows girl and boy students according to hair color.

Environmental play

The environment offers endless possibilities for scientific experimentation, for almost all age groups. A Discovery Centre can easily incorporate ecological materials that allow interesting play scenarios.

Almost all preschoolers have at some time planted seeds in a cup and then waited for them to grow — common scenarios like this can be expanded and altered in any number of interesting ways. To use the example above, different seeds can be used, or seeds can be planted in different materials (e.g., sand, clay, regular soil, or gravel). Transparent containers can be used, so children can watch roots develop. Plants can be exposed to the sun in different ways. Children can experiment with fertilizer or even introduce bugs. In all cases, teachers should encourage the children to make up their own minds about what is happening and to reach their own conclusions. Although these activities require patience and time, the children involved will find them satisfying.

Other environmental lessons can be gained through play scenarios, too. Simple experiments that imitate weather effects, like water and soil erosion, are easy for children to set up and fascinating for them to undertake. Older children can set up mini-ecosystems, perhaps something like an earthworm farm in a large jar. The development of such systems is diverting and imparts important lessons about life cycles. They do it, however, in a way that draws children into a wider understanding of the interdependence of life.

Chemistry play

Not many educators or parents would be eager to address chemistry experiments, particularly for young children. With this said, young children enjoy simple chemistry experiments, easily repeated, with cheap and easily obtainable materials. For example, on the Internet there are recipes for "slime," using liquid food starch and some school white glue. Add food coloring, and watch children's delight at combining disparate materials into something else entirely. Another favorite involves adding vinegar to baking soda, creating a mini-volcano.

Simple non-cooking recipes can also show how substances of a disparate nature combine to form something useful, or at least different. Children's silly side can be engaged by checking different materials for absorbency — say, a piece of denim versus a diaper, or water versus ketchup. Remember, as with the rest of our examples, the more the experiments relate to the children's lives and the more fun they have, the greater the likelihood the lessons learned will last longer.

In the feature below, Christine Maclean, an early childhood consultant, reflects on the role of encouragement and opportunity in the development of creative problem solvers. She also reinforces the need for students to develop problem-solving skills.

The Benefits of Open-Ended Play

When my own child was around five years old, he spent the better part of day watching and collecting snails while he played outdoors. Later in the day he asked me to help him draw a snail. Ordinarily, my first response would be to show him how to do it but, for whatever reason, this time I didn't. I asked him to try it himself, and then I sat back and watched what happened. He made a number of attempts to sketch the spiral shape of a snail shell, each attempt becoming more and more complex and each time becoming closer and closer to a recognizable snail shape. I felt like I was able to see those little wheels spinning in his head as he figured out how to solve this problem. He ended up with an accurate representation of a snail but, more important, he ended up with a sense of real accomplishment because he was able to solve his problem by himself.

He has since grown up to be a wonderfully creative artist and an innovative problem solver who has learned to rely on his own ability to generate solutions to life's situations. I'm not saying that every child who is able to figure things out for himself will grow up to be an artist or an innovator, but I can guarantee that if children aren't given opportunities for open-ended play activities, there won't be nearly the number of artists and innovators that this next generation will need in order to deal with the multitude of problems that our generation has bestowed upon them.

— Christine Maclean

Outdoor play

"Parks are fun when you're with your friends and people of your own age."
— Child quoted in the 2009 British Playday study

The playground, yard, or park also makes an excellent site for scientific play. Here are examples of outdoor play that may lead to further explorations:

- Playground games can be altered to include scientific principles; for example, have children form a solar system, even including comets and asteroids!
- The swings and slide can be used to measure gravity's effects, using different-sized children as the tests.
- Outdoor collecting games (e.g., pebbles, wildflowers, and different leaves) teach children about their own environment in a playful way.
- The playground is a perfect spot for experimenting with paper-plane designs, materials, and propulsion.
- On a snowy day, have children examine snowflakes, perhaps looking for ones that are the same . . .
- Make a sundial out of sticks and stones to tell time.
- Smell different flowers. Which ones do the children like or dislike?
- Construct a long-distance phone from paper cups and a lengthy piece of string. Playing with this is as interesting to children now as it was a hundred years ago.
- Set up a backyard weather station, and record daily temperatures and rainfall. Are they the same as elsewhere?

Children love to explore and play outside. If educators recognize this and use their own skills and interests to include science ideas in the play, the play will be both effective and resonant. The possibilities are endless.

Science in the early years is about experiencing the physical world in many forms. It is a hands-on, discovery process of learning, whereby children come up with their own suppositions about what they see. Through play-based learning centres, such as the Discovery Centre, children can engage all of their senses to create new language that can communicate both their feelings and understandings.

Many studies suggest that children are becoming disconnected from the natural environment due to urban living, technology, and generally busy lives. This disconnect, in turn, can become a disassociation with the natural world and inhibit their curiosity and questions about the world. Although the limited space, time, and resources of the classroom may make science play a challenge, the benefits to children in becoming creative risk takers and problem solvers make it well worth the effort.

6

Technology, Computers, and Play

Technology is ubiquitous in the daily lives of young children today. It is not unusual for children as young as three to have mastered TV remote controls, loading and unloading compact disc players, or uploading favorite computer games. Toy stores are full of elaborate electronic games (many touting dubious educational outcomes), while any gathering of little boys will find at least a few buried in hand-held video games, like the immensely popular Nintendo DS.

Although many teachers and parents are uncomfortable with the amount of technology present in children's lives, it need not be seen as a threat or a hindrance to educational progress. Parents can readily use the technology in the home to create playful scenarios that are both enjoyable and instructive. As educators, we have a responsibility to help children become comfortable with technology, so that they can learn to use it properly and safely. For the purpose of this book, when we discuss children's play and technology, the primary area of concern for both educators and parents is the computer and its close relatives.

Handled properly, computers and other screen-based technological tools can enhance children's cognitive development. The key is finding play scenarios in which children are active participants, learning through the play, rather than just passively working their way through endless levels of pointless games. Realistically, computers and computer-based technology are going to remain a significant part of children's lives — the goal is to use them to enhance children's educational needs.

Video Games and Their Benefits

An article about the European Union study can be found at this site: http://www.guardian.co.uk/technology/2009/feb/12/computer-games-eu-study.

A popular myth is that video games and the like are just plain bad for children; however, recent studies by child psychologists suggest that *what* children are playing on the screen is a much more crucial measure of good or bad. A widely cited European Union study, which looked at young children throughout Europe, concluded that "video games can stimulate learning of facts and skills such as strategic thinking, creativity, cooperation and innovative thinking, which are important skills in the information society."

Games that promote positive social, emotional, and intellectual outcomes, enjoyed in moderation (and not to the exclusion of other types of play), are likely to be no more harmful than any other sort of play. Since the same cannot be said about violent and aggressive games, we will focus our attention here on positive

tive play situations (see PBS's Video Game Revolution site, which includes "Eight Myths about Video Games Debunked" by Henry Jenkins).

My work in digital reading and children's play in virtual worlds points to some of the benefits and sense of reality that can come from playing computer games. In the following anecdote, that sense of reality becomes intertwined with a child's feeling of responsibility.

> *Seven-year-old Adam was talking about feeding his family's dogs, a simple chore he much enjoyed, when suddenly his happy-go-lucky features clouded over.*
>
> *"We have to play Webkinz today," he said urgently. "We need to feed our animals. They will be getting hungry too."*
>
> *It had been several days since we had entered the virtual world of Webkinz together, where his small collection of stuffed toys seemed to lead a real existence. As part of the game, in a given session, players assumed the identity of one of the toys from their own collection of toys. Feeding these animals a virtual treat was a treasured part of Adam's computer play. In his mind, the needs of his fictional Webkinz were as urgent and important as those of the family's puppies.*

How Children Interact with Computers

Getting children to interact with technology is not difficult — almost all children love to play with computers — but understanding *how* children interact with computers is harder. Teachers and educators need to understand how children learn when they encounter computer programs and their like and keep these learning processes well in mind when directing children's computer interactions. Researchers Jane Davidson and June Wright (1994) have divided the learning process into four stages:

1. *Discovery:* The child experiences a growing awareness that what appears on the screen is what the child has created or selected.
2. *Involvement:* The child becomes motivated to learn and master basic commands and sequences.
3. *Self-Confidence:* The child learns to complete plans and to predict outcomes.
4. *Creativity:* The child invents his or her own solutions to problems, can design challenges for others, and can even create original scenarios.

As children move through these stages, whether in the space of five minutes or a year, they are in a very real way learning to use computers as tools, just like a box of crayons or a bag of construction blocks. If we as educators think this way, we will be better able to successfully create a space for computer use in children's play.

Educators and parents will also realize that close supervision must be an important part of any such play experiences. We cannot expect children to use any discretion, find safe and stimulating play scenarios, or monitor their time interacting with technology. Although many studies stress the positive side of computer games, almost all also agree on a policy of moderation. Hours spent interacting with a screen provide no substitute for other sorts of play. To use a metaphor, you would not feed a child exclusively on one type of fruit or vegetable. Neither should a child's play be dominated by the computer screen. Software and websites must be carefully chosen, to be both stimulating from a play perspective but also to be full of both positive messages and useful learning moments. Every child will be different — some children will easily master games and sites that require strong literacy skills; others will be more visually oriented and will gravitate towards games that flatter those skills. As we all know, boys and girls are often drawn to very different types of play, and as is the case on the playground, so will it be on the screen.

Discovery-Oriented Computer Play

A number of studies agree that discovery-oriented programs are often the best choices for computer play. These programs involve children in step-by-step play and are open-ended in terms of their outcomes. Historically, such programs were the preserve of expensive software games. Today, computer games are being divided into two categories. In the home, they use dedicated computers, like Sony's Playstation or the Nintendo Wii. These units offer a wide variety of games, almost all of which require the user to become part of an immersive environment. Educational outcomes are often implicit. In the classroom, anecdotal evidence suggests that conventional educational software is being steadily supplanted by online games, which offer a wide variety of free play opportunities.

These programs will often exist in self-contained virtual worlds, known as "micro-worlds," which operate with rule structures and precepts easily understandable to children. An example of such a game environment is that found on the wildly popular www.webkinz.com. The Webkinz world, based on a popular stuffed toy, contains a number of games and interactive activities aimed at children from several different age groups. While not explicitly educational, the Webkinz world does call upon basic literacy and math skills, and the care of the player's virtual pets requires the child to understand responsibility and other life skills. Like many such programs, the repetition of the game allows the child to gain virtual money or other credits, which then can be used to alter the game's physical makeup. Even very young children are fascinated by this make-believe economy, where they can be active participants in a way impossible in their real lives. In the game, they have total control of their avatars; they are allowed to make choices and discover how these choices can be both positive and negative.

As illustrated below, my research with seven-year-old Adam describes how some of his choices led to an unwelcomed consequence and a life lesson.

While Adam and I were playing in the Webkinz world, I was distracted by a message from another researcher. For a few minutes Adam played on his own, while I dealt with the issue from nearby. After a few minutes had passed, I could see he was getting frustrated.

"What's wrong?" *I asked him.*

"All my money's gone," *he said sadly.*

During my lapse in supervision, he had entered the world's virtual store and used all his game credits on a series of purchases for his avatar's make-believe "room." These included a mini-UFO, a working toilet, and a snowman, all objects of great interest to him. He was disappointed to discover that he now had no credits for any other purchases.

"Sorry," *I explained.* "Once you spend all your game money, it's all gone. You made your own choices on what to buy, remember."

"I know," *he said.* "My mom says stuff like that to me all the time in the candy store."

The game had reinforced one of Adam's important life lessons: spend your money wisely.

Other such programs may allow collaboration between children or allow them to create shared environments.

It is also worth noting here that few young children will be much excited by the sorts of educational games that are just old-fashioned classroom worksheets disguised by rudimentary animation or encouraging messages. Although such games are useful tools for older children who need reinforcement in specific skills, even younger ones can easily distinguish between play and regular school-work; they will not likely engage in such programs in a creative fashion unless made to do so by an educator or parent.

Criteria for Assessing Computer Games

The list of games and websites is endless; it changes constantly, as sites come in and out of fashion, become popular, and, in turn, are displaced by something new. So it is with the games themselves. Computer technology changes so quickly that a piece of software that was cutting edge for last year's class will be stiff and clumsy for this year's students. It would be better, perhaps, for educators to think hard about a specific game or site, and ask, "What will the child be getting out of it?" If the answer seems to be nothing more than amusement, then it is time to move on. Otherwise, educators may be wise to adopt some of the following criteria:

- *Is the software fun?* If the children do not feel like they are playing, it will not work on any level.
- *Is it suited to their ages and skills?* Just because it features a familiar cartoon character does not mean it will be suitable.
- *Can the students understand the goals?* They have to feel a sense of accomplishment in the game environment if any other educational purposes are to be established.
- *Will the game allow pretend play?* If a game does not engage children's creativity and imagination in some fashion, it will probably have only limited appeal.
- *Can the software platform accommodate more than one child? Can they return to their own space in the game?* Most computer games allow a child to "save" his or her own character or accomplishments, something that children find valuable and important.
- *Will the game allow collaboration between students, or small groups of students?* Cooperation is a vital skill in any group of young children, and games that promote it will prove useful in a classroom setting.
- *Does the game get harder as the children become more experienced?* Better games expand and grow more difficult as the children get better at them.
- *Will the software allow a degree of trial and error?* Games that perfect this aspect will develop the children's own intuitiveness.
- *Is the game too easy?* Games that constantly reward a child with compliments or credit without any real accomplishment are of little educational value.
- *Is the game too fast?* Many computer games rely on sophisticated animation and effects. Children often need time to think about and process tasks — the game should allow this.

- *What are the societal values of the game? Does it promote fairness, gender balance, and tolerance?* This can be a delicate area. While few children's sites will be obviously flawed, games are often full of stereotypes that can easily go unrecognized. Educators need to be mindful of subtle messages buried in the game's characters and nuances.
- *Will children sympathize with and relate to the characters?* For example, few boys will wish to be seen playing a princess game (at least while under the scrutiny of their fellows), no matter how much fun it is. Similarly, a game based on a character perceived as being the purview of younger children will be discarded quickly.

And, most important of all,

- *Have you played the game yourself?* No child, either in a classroom or at home, should be exposed to a game or website until the adult has thoroughly explored and tested it.

Learning with Interactive Technology

The teaching reflection that ends this chapter recognizes that nothing is more authentic to children than computers and television. Kindergarten teacher Carrie Collins shares how technology, including interactive whiteboards, can enhance the teaching of important concepts, such as letter-and-sound recognition and self.

Technology in the Classroom

Children learn when they have the opportunity to communicate, to question, and to reflect on their thinking, while seeing how they can make connections to what they already know — one thing children already know is how to play. As a Kindergarten teacher, I encourage the development of thinking and learning skills by engaging children in meaningful and purposeful learning experiences that connect to their own lives. Nothing is more authentic to children than television and computers, which is why children as young as five years old easily adapt to using interactive whiteboards, such as the SMART Board.

From fingers in the air to interactive whiteboard

One key concept for the Kindergarten student is letter-and-sound recognition. Students need to know not only how to say their ABCs, but they also need to know what sounds the letters make, what the letters look like, and how to print these letters. I dedicate a full week on one letter, using the "Writing without Tears" formula for letter development.

First, I model on chart paper how to form the letter, and my students use their fingers to draw the letter in the air on imaginary giant paper. I then demonstrate the sound the letter makes, asking my students to repeat the sound. We discuss the part of the mouth the sound came from and whether they have to use their teeth, tongue, or breath to make the sound. We then brainstorm all the words that start with that letter of the week.

My students are then given playdough to form the letter. This is done in two different ways: the students roll out the playdough like a long snake and form the shape of the letter; or, usually on day two of our week, they roll the playdough flat and trace the shape of the letter into the dough with a finger or pencil.

My students then have the opportunity to use our interactive whiteboard to write the letter on the board. I take this moment for assessment, using the recording feature. I am able to record what my students write on the board, to determine if they are forming the letter properly. The students then click on their letter to hear its sounds. Eventually, this work leads into learning sight words, where my students play with the fridge letter magnets and the fridge magnet application on the SMART Board, dragging the letters to form letter combinations and words. This is often done in centres in combination with the playdough activities.

Multi-media portfolios on the self

Another key concept in Kindergarten is self. Using our interactive whiteboard and programs like Kidspiration, Notebook, Paint, and Photostory 3, I work with my students to create an "All about Me" portfolio with scanned or e-mailed pictures, drawn representations, and/or simple words. Parents are invited to contribute to their child's project, sharing pictures and audio files. I also have my students use a microphone and the Audacity program to comment on their own lives, often times pretending they are news reporters.

This is the video-game generation of children. They have grown up with television and computers, so completing their work using these media is both fun and meaningful for them.

Connecting with students' everyday lives

The way I teach allows my students to use what they know to be a part of their everyday lives. Interactive whiteboards allow them to make observations and record characteristics, similarities, differences, and changes. They also let them create story webs and Venn diagrams, and classify materials, events, and phenomena (e.g., sort according to simple criteria such as color and size).

The side effect to this form of diverse learning is that my students not only have the opportunity to meet the desired learning outcomes in a cross-curricular manner, but they also acquire technology skills, including the proper use of a computer, keyboard, and mouse. They learn what and what not to do with a SMART Board — for example, not to use a regular pen or marker and how to touch the screen. They also learn how to use specific resources with the SMART Board, including a flatbed scanner, how to print, how to load a CD/DVD, and how to log on to the Internet.

— Carrie Collins

Experiences described in this chapter speak to our need to be educators conscious of the choices we make and the offerings of particular games and sites. As educators, we must constantly seek positive ways to use technology, while also reaching towards balance, taking into account the lives children lead at home and elsewhere. Technology will likely be a big part of children's lives, but it should be balanced with all the other elements in their play explorations.

7

English Language Learning through Play

As the primary occupation of children during their early years, play is able to integrate a number of aspects of the developing child, including the child's intellectual, cultural, social, physical, and creative inclinations. By its nature, play is free flowing, determined by the interests of the child. Children's play is improved if they have a wide variety of experiences to draw upon and if they have the ability to communicate these experiences and ideas to others. The better their social skills, the better they are likely to communicate, and the more they will benefit from play.

Fostering Educational Play

The lighter the hand of the guiding adult, the more motivated and spontaneous the play is likely to be. Researcher Barry Milne (1997) would go so far as to argue that "educational play in early childhood is neither play nor education. It is not play . . . if it is guided by an adult; neither is it educational in a rich sense if it lacks any adult guidance." In other words, when we use play to enhance children's education, we have to be careful about what sort of play we are encouraging. For a child, play and fun are one and the same. In order to maximize play's learning potential, we need to examine what children are doing when they play and then use this knowledge to further our understanding about learning in the classroom.

Recognizing the potential of symbolic play

In their early years, most children enjoy imaginative, or symbolic, play, where one thing is used to stand for or represent another. It can range from a child's simple imitation of adult actions — say, cooking and cleaning — to more elaborate fantasy scenarios, whereby household objects stand in for unicorns and castles. Symbolic play is vital for the development of representational and abstract thought. Early in their thinking, children rely on shared experiences. Through symbolic play they begin to process and understand events and scenarios that are in the past or the future, or are completely imaginary (Bruner, 1990).

The influential Russian psychologist Lev Vygotsky saw symbolic play as one of the first steps towards oral language and literacy — after all, languages are, first and foremost, a way of verbally representing the life we see around us. Vygotsky was fond of imaginative play, as it allows children to perform at a higher level; the context of such play is akin to the forms of knowing children experience. It brings them to a state where they can reach beyond the concrete world of the here and now and instead play and imagine places, times, and scenarios not bound by their play space.

Encouraging the development of children's play

To take this into the realm of literacy development, we can look at the seminal work of Carol Taylor Schrader (see Schrader, 1999). She agrees with Vygotsky's theories, arguing that symbolic play is ideal for literacy development. Schrader prefers guided play scenarios, whereby the adult participates in the play, becoming part of the child's framework, but does not plan or otherwise direct it. The adult's role is to encourage the development of the play, with the goal being to expand its ideas, and to get the children to contribute as much as possible.

A problem is that the current trend in early childhood education is to emphasize earlier and earlier textual literacy, usually at the expense of playing. Play-based programs have been abandoned in favor of structured educational programs. More often than not, children are passive participants in such programs, which see them as receptacles waiting to be filled with knowledge. Parents of children aged four to six are surrounded by media messages encouraging them to purchase all manner of early literacy toys and texts, all of which promise to have the child reading impeccably at a very young age. Spontaneous play is not part of the "schedule."

Symbols in play and in literacy

Yet researchers such as Howard Gardner believe that play is the very basis for literacy. Gardner's research has revealed that the creative processes inherent in play are the same that create literacy. This theory starts from the realization that symbols represent something, either an object, an event, or an idea. Words are also symbols. Whether we are adults or children, our thinking skills involve the manipulation of words — and ergo, symbols — as we use words, numbers, images, and notations to describe the world around us. The foundations of these manipulations are the real beginnings of literacy, *not* necessarily a child's first experiences with books.

Symbols are a real part of even the smallest child's play, even when not verbalized. Drawing, modeling-clay, painting, make-believe play — they all require the use of symbols. These symbols are, in turn, transformed into linguistic expressions, which then form the basis for oral and textual literacy.

It is interesting to note that during play, children can use complex forms of language. They use a larger vocabulary, which necessitates longer utterances than they might use in another context. These are important attributes of play for later literacy development.

Play, Literacy, and English Language Learners

Imaginative, interactive, and collaborative play situations and scenarios are ideal for children who are learning English as another language. They can provide a safe and engaging way for them to practise and use a new language. Children are very motivated to develop relationships with others. When engaged in play, they can develop language in a time and space that suits their needs rather than those of the classroom or household.

"Play is indeed a life-saving gift. . . . It allows you to be anything that you want to be, to do anything that you want to do and to have fun. Should it be given rather than a gift? Is it not the right of a child to be able to play?"
— Dr. Linda Cameron

It is important for the educator to remember, however, that children from different cultural backgrounds come with different sets of experiences — the symbols they have developed to describe their worlds will differ greatly from those of native English speakers. Nor can we assume that western theories of play will necessarily apply to ELL students. Most of the theories about play we rely on come from western studies, and our collective wisdom is dominated by our own experience in an English-speaking world. Some cultures value the role of play in children's lives; others do not. Adult participation in fostering play may or may not be required, encouraged, or apparent.

Educators who work with young English language learners need to be aware of their students' cultural differences and the cultural beliefs of the parents. Some ELL families will just be settling in their new country, and the values of the old country will be strong and will dominate parents' view of their children's education. Some customs will be modified, some will be cherished, and others may conflict with the educator's approach.

Nonetheless, it is important to remember the results of researchers like Anca Nemoianu, who has made extensive studies of ELL students. Nemoianu convincingly demonstrated that children learn another language faster and with less effort during play, especially if they are trying to establish friendships with peers. Her research has been borne out by U.K. researchers Iram Siraj-Blatchford and Priscilla Clarke who also draw a link between the motivations of social play and children's ability to quickly master a new language.

Researcher Lily Wong Fillmore (1976) noted that children hear many phrases in a repetitive context during play, thereby making the phrases easier to learn. In my own experience, I saw this finding played out in my home community, as I watched a vivacious four-year-old boy in my child's preschool go from almost zero English to a functional use of the language in just six months of companionable play.

Early childhood educators have a particularly valuable role in the play of English language learners. As they would for children with different economic backgrounds or physical abilities, they need to encourage all their students to cross these boundaries. All children need opportunities to express themselves through play, and professional educators have a critical opportunity to make this happen. While we earlier expressed doubts about adults guiding the play, this does not mean that adults cannot take part in it. Educators should not shy away from becoming involved in such play, particularly where they see opportunities to support language development.

In the following feature, Julia Billard shares her first efforts to promote in her Kindergarten students an appreciation of diversity and a respect for the many different cultures represented in her classroom.

"I like to play with my friends at recess and when we get extra play time for being good."
— Child (age 6)

One Teacher, 54 Students: Crossing Cultural Boundaries

Two weeks upon graduation, I travelled to Fort McMurray, Alberta, a town in the midst of an oil boom, bursting with new arrivals from across Canada and around the world. I walked into the District office on a Monday morning and by the next day I was given a full-time position as a Kindergarten teacher. I met with the principal and was given my class list — 54 students. "Wow" was my first thought, and my second was "I can't wait to meet the other teacher."

There was no other teacher. I was the only teacher for 54 five-year-olds.

I met with my 54 families — turns out that around 20 of them were ESL (English as a Second Language) students. Some of these students were fairly fluent in English, half spoke broken English, and one spoke no English at all. My classroom was like a garden salad of cultures, religions, and languages — and I was the spoon that had to keep everything mixing, blending, and moving. Many of my students' families had just moved to Canada, and neither parent nor child could really understand a word I was going to say.

I decided to make a conscious effort to keep placing myself in my students' situations. Would I be interested in listening to a story read in another language? How would I feel if everything I knew was uprooted and I had moved to this new English-speaking country where everyone talked and looked differently? Kindergarten was supposed to be fun and educational, but I couldn't even draw upon prior knowledge — I had none!

I wanted my students to embrace their home cultures and identities so in early October, we held a Multicultural Day. All of my students wore or brought something that represented their culture. I wore a T-shirt from my home in Newfoundland, played some music from my own tradition, and taught the students how to dance a Newfoundland jig. Parents were also encouraged to join us, and many brought traditional foods like samosas and Ukrainian perogies. The highlight of the day was when a very shy student, originally from India, taught the class a Bollywood-inspired dance.

I remember stopping to look around at my class that day, seeing everyone together, and realizing that it didn't matter if you were from Japan, India, the Philippines, Pakistan, Guyana, or Canada. Children are children, no matter where they are from in the world. They should be taught that their identity and culture make them unique; however, they also need to try new things, hear new music, and taste new foods. It was definitely an entertaining day, but most important, everyone went home knowing more about and respectful of different cultures. Even if some students didn't quite understand what I was saying, their smiles and laughter spoke volumes.

— Julia Billard

Scaffolding Play for ELL Students

The makeup of a given group of children will have a significant impact on the ultimate success of English language learners (just as it will have an impact on gender roles and socio-economic divisions). Educators can easily affect the makeup of these groups without becoming heavy-handed. We can readily encourage children who are fluent in English to mingle with those who are not.

A number of simple classroom games particularly lend themselves to groups of children that include both ELL students and native English speakers.

Picture Bingo: In this game, children match pictures held up by the bingo caller to the words on their bingo cards. To help them with the words, the bingo caller can describe the chosen picture as a place, person, object, or whatever, thus making the game fair and informative for all.

Snap and Simple Card Games, such as Old Maid and Crazy Eights: Snap, to use one example, is a high-speed matching game, one likely to be more popular among boys and competitive students, no matter their language proficiency.

Snakes and Ladders: This simple board game requires no textual understanding other than the numbers on dice or a spinning wheel. With its sudden rewards and disasters, it appeals to children's sense of humor.

Jigsaw Puzzles: Encourage a group of children with different language abilities to work together on a puzzle. Choosing a puzzle of fewer than 100 pieces keeps young children interested and not easily frustrated. The key is for children to feel success.

Counting Games: Simple counting games — for example, how many children have long hair? how many are wearing something brown? — can be geared to suit children of all language abilities.

Matching Games: Almost all western children have played matching games that involve turning over a series of cards to reveal which ones match. Cards that carry images, numbers, letters, or whatever can be chosen.

Games like these provide many opportunities for children to form sequences, ask questions, put labels on objects, take turns, and most important, have fun in their new environment. They can be played in English, in another language, or in a combination of languages. Encourage children to make the language learning two-way — while the ELL students are learning English, invite them to share their first language with other students.

Resources That Honor Diversity

Supporting an environment that honors diversity needs to be at the centre of planning for the ELL classroom or early childhood education centre. Play resources, decorations, toys, and other materials all need to be chosen with this precept in mind. These resources, whatever they are, will often be the starting point for the children's spontaneous play or for play scenarios organized by the educator. We are talking primarily about the interior environment, but can also encompass the playground and other outdoor spaces.

Here are some classroom ideas that can become the foundation for play scaffolding:

Home Corner: A home corner should be a space that encourages children to share family cultural practices, such as making dinner, or activities, such as holding a game night. Here, the various cultures represented by English language learners in the classroom are celebrated. Dolls make a simple way to demonstrate diversity, as do pictures, food labels in a different language, or cultural artifacts like chopsticks. Aspects of the home corner should be chosen so as to encourage sharing by the English language learners, and curiosity and explorations by the English speakers.

Class Multilingual Library: Thanks to the Internet, it is now possible to obtain texts from just about anywhere, or at least reasonable facsimiles of them. If resources allow, create a small multilingual library that incorporates the home languages of the class's students. Doing this will have several possible (and positive) outcomes. First of all, it demonstrates to the ELL students that despite the necessity of learning English, their home language is still important and valued.

It also demonstrates to other children that a peer's language is not "wrong" but as legitimate as English. When the parents of ELL students see their own language validated, they may feel encouraged to become involved in the literacy pursuits of their children. In an ideal situation, books printed in several languages could be obtained, thus maximizing cultural exchange and multilingual efforts. These stories can, in turn, spur role-playing and other play scenarios.

It is important to take a careful look at the English resources that may be placed in the class library. For example, be sure to consider whether children of a different race are always illustrated in a rural or tribal setting — it is easy for stereotypes to become established among young children. Take some care to avoid unnecessary stereotypes when choosing pictorial materials. Educators need to be aware and wary that text materials provide a suitably diverse view of the world.

Storytime: Storytime, a part of most early classroom experiences, can also be fine-tuned for ELL situations. Careful selection will allow educators to utilize books with minimal text, but highly evocative illustrations. While reading a story in another language may not be practical for all, it is something to consider. If nothing else, it would give English language speakers some sympathy for the plight of the English language learner who arrives with little or no facility in English. As you would with any group of children, make an effort to engage children of different backgrounds, interests, and comprehension abilities.

Role Playing: Some role-playing games are "user friendly," as it were, for language speakers from different backgrounds. For example, a class could imitate different animals or act out simple activities such as household chores. Doing this would allow children with limited language abilities to participate fully in a play scenario.

Interactive Rhymes: Poems are a simple but effective way to assist English language learners. Finger plays such as "One potato, two potato" and "One, two, buckle my shoe" are good for teaching the concept of counting. Language is taught through repetition, and this principle can be extended to the ELL classroom with great success. Hand-clapping rhymes such as "B-i-n-g-o," "Miss Mary Mac," or even "Say Say Oh Playmate" are popular with older children, as are tongue twisters and other funny and playful spoken-word games.

Music Games: Music is universal, and even the shyest ELL students may come to life when they hear a song in their first language. Music can be used in a number of ways to enhance play scenarios for ELL students. Thanks to the Internet, a child-friendly listening post is simply created, using MP3s that incorporate songs from many lands and languages. Simple play songs can help students to become involved in games: we may take for granted that everyone knows such songs as "Ring around the Rosie" or "London Bridge," but they can play an invaluable role in involving ELL students with the wider classroom activity.

A good idea is to encourage in English language learners an understanding that people of different genders, races, and physical abilities all have an equal role in our society. Examples include girls playing sports, men taking a role in domestic life, women working in a trade, and people of different cultures interacting. Looking through newspapers and local community bulletins would show children how everyone has an equal role when contributing to the community. Children can be encouraged to cut out pictures and newspaper headings that celebrate the different roles people play in the community.

What to Consider When Involving ELL Students in Play

ELL students' learning of English is undoubtedly enhanced by playing with native or other English-speaking children. Educators who promote this, either by leading or creating play opportunities and scenarios, would be wise to consider the following ideas:

- Certain children are outgoing and risk taking; others are not. Groups should include children of both types and offer opportunities to all.
- Children have different language abilities: some will learn quickly; others will take much longer.
- Motivation will vary widely, as will parental support.
- The play possibilities that the environment offers will greatly affect potential outcomes.
- Diversity in all its appearances, including through texts, visuals, and playmaking scenarios, is a necessary part of the ELL experience.
- English must be seen as important, without diminishing or dismissing children's home languages.
- As much as possible, communicate with, reassure, and involve parents — they may not understand why or what play is doing in the classroom.

Welcoming children who come to school with another language can be a challenge; however, it can be met through positive interactions. Keep in mind that language growth is stimulated when a variety of the children's interests are engaged. Having the home share in the child's school experiences can provide you with many points of connection. Some teachers, like Julia Billard, have created Books about Me with their English language learner students so that the students can share their talents and interests with classmates. Through my classroom observations, I have learned that English language learners first need to be able to trust their teachers, if they are to gain the confidence necessary to learn a new language. A key element in building this trust is to create many opportunities for children to feel successful right from the start of their classroom experiences.

ELL teachers are often discomfited by their students' silence, but they need not be. Respect this silence as a time when the students are practising listening skills and gaining confidence in learning about language. Language is not just about the words we use to communicate but also about how to use particular words in certain situations. Enabling children to play in small groups will provide valuable opportunities for the development of both language and social skills needed for the early-grade classroom.

8

Building Citizenship through Child Play

As children play in their physical environment, they learn how to use their world to advantage. One of the greatest aspects of true free play is that it allows children to learn and to take risks in a safe environment. Safe learning, in turn, builds self-confidence. For example, on a playground's climbing equipment, children are able to test their physical limits in a relatively risk-free environment, exercising those skills until they have mastered them.

When my own son was mastering his sliding technique on the small playground near our house, his constant shouts of "Watch me again, Mommy," were not just about showing off. He was testing his abilities and challenging his physical limitations. His repeated actions — and my many, many affirmations — were all part of the long process of building his self-confidence. From such free play, children learn to take risks, solve problems, and expand their horizons.

Many parents practise these self-confidence building tactics instinctively, so most children come to school with a great sense of accomplishment upon which teachers can build. We want to create a positive reflection of children's abilities; in turn, self-confident learners contribute to building a classroom where collaborative learning flourishes. Children will develop positive attitudes that encourage them to become active citizens and partake in collaborative decision making. Active citizenship that is responsive to the needs of our society begins when teachers engage children in collaborative learning activities: skills developed from such activities draw upon children's understanding of social responsibility and ask children to critically think about how their actions affect the well-being of others and the community.

Helping children to understand who they are and how they can contribute to a healthy community is important in building their social, cognitive, and emotional well-being. Forming positive relationships in early years' classrooms where children can explore their feelings, talk about concerns, and express their opinions enhances their self-confidence and self-esteem. Children need to become skilled in how they use language to communicate ideas and express emotions — doing so will help build a collaborative classroom and contribute to a healthy community.

We must remember that children understand their world based on what they have learned in the home. For example, many children in our society learn at an early age about the tooth fairy, a mythical being who exchanges money for baby teeth. While English-speaking Canadian children probably accept this belief, when they get to school they may encounter other beliefs. For example, in many Latin countries baby teeth are exchanged by a little mouse. Other cultures have no traditions about baby teeth, and children from such homes may find the whole thing ridiculous. The home provides a foundation of cultural reference points; whether they mean to or not, schools inevitably offer much broader perspectives.

During their early years, in their own social and cultural contexts, children form concepts about who they are and how they relate to the world around them. Helping children to develop a positive self-image, show independence, and self-regulate is done within the context of the home and in early years' classrooms. Through the development of valuable interpersonal skills, children learn to communicate their opinions and thoughts. A positive self-image provides a child with the confidence and independence that bring forth critical and creative skills which lead to social competence and emotional intelligence. Children learn to take responsibility for themselves and others.

This chapter looks at what it means to develop a child's positive understanding of self and others, and recommends skills you may wish to build in children. The activities shared in this chapter help to create a collaborative learning classroom that moves students closer to understanding the importance of citizenship.

Developing Understanding of Community

Children become aware of what it means to be a part of a community at a young age. They understand that a community can be a playgroup, their classmates, or a family. Community has both social and cultural aspects; it is a huge part of the way we communicate and create meaningful experiences in our lives.

For children, their engagement in a community gives them a chance to communicate, to learn, and to contribute to something that matters. Playmaking creates many opportunities for this sort of learning to be explored. Here is an example.

Each morning, in Sue-Ann Carter's Grade 1 class, the boys share their Pokémon cards. Because they find the nuances of the proper game too complex to grasp, they have created a simple version of the game, which involves trading cards with similar images. Most girls in the class have little or no interest in the game, the preserve of the class's young boys. For the several weeks in which the game maintains their collective interest, they call the daily game sessions the "Pokémon Club," loudly proclaiming their membership. In other words, they have formed a community, one based on their creation and enjoyment of a card game.

Being a part of something means having special beliefs and values. Teaching young children to become aware of the world in which they make meaning requires that they develop skills in which their voices and actions have both meaning and consequence at the same time. Learning what it means to be a good citizen requires the development of communication skills, expressions of viewpoints and opinions, listening and empathy with others, and situations being shared. In a classroom, this may be as simple as children's perceptions of how they are to behave. Understanding how positive choices contribute to a school community and how negative choices lead to misunderstandings and conflict can assist children in understanding what it means to contribute to the classroom and communities in which they live.

Building Blocks to Community

Building on the foundations of community and empathy for others helps children to understand the organization of their community, the dynamics of families, and how people all contribute to our democracy. While these concepts are somewhat weighty, they are well within the grasp of even very young children, if offered to them in a fashion to which they can relate.

School communities strive to have children see themselves within a larger world and what that means within a diverse society. Developing an appreciation for the differences in others should lead to an acceptance of others' opinions and respect for viewpoints that may be different from children's own. As young learners develop socially, cognitively, and emotionally, it is necessary that they understand everyone has rights and responsibilities within a community. Accepting and celebrating many cultures, and creating a basic perception of equality, are also important. Developing children's emotional maturity and healthy self-image helps children make positive choices and celebrate the diversity in our world — they first come to accept themselves and then learn to take responsibility for each other.

Identity is formed at an early age, and a name is probably the first way in how the child defines who he or she is. Children need to understand that the names of others are representative of who they are, too. Names are chosen through practised customs — they may have personal, cultural, or religious significance. Using children's first names is a good way to build respect and to introduce positive ideas about identity and self-identification within the classroom. (See "Play with names" in Chapter 3.)

Engaged learners, responsible citizens

In order to evolve into socially and morally responsible citizens, children need to be prepared with the skills of active and engaged learners. Building such foundations on their sense of what community and responsibility mean places them in a world where they can act with confidence and commitment, with an understanding of the positive difference they can make.

Creating a peaceful school with a student body whose members are respectful of one another is part of the growth of a healthy community of learners. We have all been on a playground and have heard the names that children give to others who may be different or have seen how some children are excluded for reasons unknown to adults. At the same time, we teachers and parents often have cause to notice how refined young students' sense of justice is. We need to be able to build on this sense so that children may become aware that their actions affect the well-being of others — even in a global sense, we need for children to care for the earth by recognizing their responsibility for a share of it. Through learning how to think critically and problem-solve, children come to understand that their own efforts to provide solutions are a way in which community may be created.

Classroom play on collective responsibility

One of the best ways to enhance children's sense of responsibility for their own community is through a play-acting game, What Happens Next? The children are given a scenario and are asked to play-act what should happen next. After one or two children act out a given scenario, the rest could be asked their opinions, something that builds their critical thinking and problem-solving skills.

A key element of each scenario is that some clear moral or responsible action should be indicated. The teacher need not pass judgment on the outcome, as the children will usually figure out the best course of action. The scenarios can be simple for younger children or more elaborate for older ones. Here are some suggestions:

- As a child, you find a brand-new toy on the school playground.
- You start eating your lunch, only to discover that it is someone else's.
- Everyone in class is going to get into trouble for something you just did.
- You accidentally broke the sink in the washroom.
- You saw someone littering outside the school.

Sharing and Its Foundations

Play shapes children's beliefs about how to act in society: they learn by doing it and by observing it. One key thing we want them to learn is how to share. Classroom activities that require children to take turns, share ideas and values, respect others' feelings, and know how to conduct themselves all lead to and are part of harmonious relationships. We see these values in classrooms when children can share their ideas in a collaborative group setting. Often, though, young children need to understand what their needs really are in order to be able to share within the classroom.

While visiting one classroom, I watched a group discussion in which the classroom teacher talked about the differences between wants and needs. Creating a chart with the children, the teacher discussed needs such as food, water, and a home, as opposed to wants such as toys, holidays, and video games. Doing this provided a good opportunity for the children to both acknowledge, and to see, their own priorities laid out in front of them. The children showed an awareness of their own feelings and began to understand the feelings of other children in the group.

Discussing their way into community

Children work naturally together and enjoy sharing their understanding and perceptions of what they observe. Learning communities are developed through collaborative group discussions where problems are identified and explored. Everyday occurrences — the cancellation of a gym class, lack of supplies, a spilled drink — are problems for which children can easily provide collective solutions. Modeling language that points to problem solving will help children to understand problems, eventually inviting their opinions in a sharing circle. The discussion that follows provides an example of proactive problem solving that promotes community building.

From a Problem to the Building of Trust

In her Grade 1 class, teacher Mernia Reid expresses concern over a recess-break safety issue.

Mernia: Boys and girls, we have a problem. Does anyone know what the problem is?

Luke: I know . . . I know. Kate slipped on juice that was on the floor.

Mernia: Yes, you are right, Luke. We are sorry, Kate, that you were hurt. Of course, we do not want anyone else to get hurt; we need to find a solution to our problem, boys and girls. It is not anyone's fault — it is everyone's responsibility to keep each other safe. What do you think we should do?

At this point, Mernia asks the children to engage in problem solving. The children make suggestions: "I think we should only have juice boxes because they do not spill as much," voices Hilary, followed by Darren, who says, "I can only bring my drink in my thermos." Eric shares his feelings: "My mom says they are a waste because the box is more garbage."

Mernia decides that a list of possible ways to solve the problem may be the best solution. The children share their solutions. Sit at your desk when you eat or drink. Don't walk around. If you spill something, clean it up or get help from the teacher if you need to. Be responsible and tell the teacher you had a drink accident. Try to use a plastic container for less waste. Remind someone who has made a spill to clean it up and help that person do it. Mernia offered some silly suggestions to make the situation more playful — these the children easily rejected.

Through resolution of this classroom problem, the Grade 1 class set a routine for how to deal with what might have become a bigger problem, that of a student being hurt. Students agreed that the rules and the set routine were important, and all children felt that their ideas had been heard. Taking turns and sharing while seeking a solution to the problem also helped build trust in the community.

Making Responsible Decisions

Building collaborative learning environments requires children to develop some knowledge about how their decision making affects others. Ideas like this, as well as more esoteric ideas, like consensus, are relatively easy to demonstrate in a playful fashion.

I remember one game my own Grade 2 teacher used — it is as useful today as it was then. She asked everyone to stand next to their desks, extend their arms, and then slowly swing their arms around in a circle. Then half the class stepped forward and we did it again. In the crowded classroom it was only seconds before children began banging into each other. Our clever teacher then asked us to decide who would be allowed to swing their arms around as much as they liked and who should sit down out of the way. The ensuing debate was lively and perfectly illustrated to us what taking personal responsibility and forming a consensus felt like.

There are many other ways of achieving this, as well.

Illustrating what consensus means through a showing of hands or use of thumb up or down helps children to visually connect with decision making in a personal way. Count hands or thumbs and announce the numbers in a decision. The topic need not be important, but it should be something of interest to the children.

Inviting children to voice their thoughts and opinions is important. "It is cold today," a teacher might say. "Should we dress warmly and go out, or stay inside? What do you think?" Or, something even simpler: "Will we make paper chains or draw pictures to decorate the classroom?" Displaying decisions through either charts or other visual aids, such as pictographs, can share the different opinions that have been expressed. It also acknowledges everyone's voice.

Helping children to weigh the positive and negative effects of their decisions asks for them to look at the pros and cons. To use the examples from above, the teacher could subtly create a wider debate: "But if we go outside, some of us will be cold . . ." "We don't have enough scissors for everyone to make chains, so some of us will have to wait for a turn." The idea is to get the children thinking about their impact on the lives of others.

Using Play to Create Collaborative Communities

Asking young children to understand the importance of their contribution to the group, sharing, and creating a shared vision are part and parcel of creating a working community. The concept of collaboration (or cooperation, as it is apt to be termed in a preschool setting) is important for play-based activities. Play often depends on collaboration.

It is simple for a teacher to provide opportunities for collaborative free play, which builds these skills. Most primary teachers will already be familiar with some of the examples given here:

Blocks and Construction Toys: Instead of working on their own projects, children should be encouraged to create a collective construction — maybe a tower or wall across one end of the class. Each child would have a number of blocks or pieces to contribute to the construction as he or she saw fit.

Board Games: More so than many board games, Snakes and Ladders teaches children patience and the importance of obeying collective rules. Older children can play with the basic concept: Perhaps they could invent their own rules for the game, like every time someone lands on a ladder all the pieces move up, no matter where they are. Children are often intrigued by their ability to alter the supposed reality of the game and by the fact that their collective collaboration is required for it to work.

Jigsaw and Map Puzzles: Puzzles are ideal for creating play-based cooperation, though they probably work better with some children than others. One interesting variation is to give each child a set number of pieces and then have the children take turns placing the pieces. Doing this enforces a certain degree of give and take among the children, and enhances their collaboration.

Recently I observed how a Junior Kindergarten teacher, Lisa Deon, created moments of collaborative play in her suburban classroom. I saw how she used language to invite the children to share in the work: "I think we need to tidy up the centres. Who will help with the drama corner? And the blocks? Thank-you, Julia and Sienna. My, with us all working together, we will have this done in no time." When they were finished, she complimented the most helpful, saying, "You are great helpers — this is why we work so well together."

In helping students to build community as a cohesive group, Lisa often asks individual students to seek solutions by cooperating with others. Over and over again, and in various ways, she returns to some key questions:

- Can everybody help in some way?
- Can you help them become a part of the play?
- How are everybody's listening ears?
- What did you decide to do first?
- Who is good at this part? Can you help him/her?
- Has everyone had a turn? How can we include everyone?
- What do you like about what you did here?
- What can you improve?

Children are born with the need to feel a part of a community. The playgroup, daycare centre, or classroom will provide their first opportunity to take part in a community outside their own families. To develop as confident children, they need to feel that they are respected, that what they say is valued, and that their presence is important to the whole. Children who understand that they are a part of a community will take positive risks and can balance their decisions, which, in turn, leads to problem solving and learning to collaborate.

Connecting Children to the Environment through Play

Having children connect to the wider world in the ways we make decisions is a necessary part of this process. Protecting the environment is a huge concern for society at large, as well as our schools and communities. While the concepts may be complex, creating play scenarios in which they are explored is relatively easy.

Some of these games are very simple. One favorite of many teachers is a smelling game (which can be adapted to teach other concepts, as well). The teacher selects a number of natural substances, for example, cut grass, wildflowers, mud, tree bark, fresh fruit, and sawdust. Students take turns blindfolding one another and then trying to identify the various substances. It is fun and sensory, but it also teaches them about the variety of life.

A similar play scenario asks students to gather leaves from their immediate neighborhood and then make tracings or rubbings from them. Even very young children will be intrigued by evidence of the wide variety of natural life around them.

Simple classroom tasks can be turned into interesting games. After lunch, one teacher asked her students to put all the waste on their desks. The children then had to decide what could be recycled, what might be composted, and what would have to go to a landfill. Older students can participate in an environmental footprint quiz, where they challenge one another to remember all the ways they use energy and resources in a given day and whether or not they are doing their part to conserve (e.g., using juice boxes or reusable containers, walking or taking a bus to school, eating fruit or a packaged snack).

Recycling household objects for arts and crafts is hardly new to most teachers and students, but by challenging students to find new uses for things and to find new things to make use of, new impetus can be added to the play. I have seen this game played out in a Grade 2 class as part of a school's Earth Day activities. Some of the children came up with ingenious uses for discarded objects: picture frames made from cereal boxes, matching games made from old catalogue cutouts, and juice-box dolls were just a few.

Concepts such as global warming and water conservation do not readily lend themselves to play scenarios, but they can be introduced through games. Many teacher manuals and websites suggest play-acting and tableau games to create awareness of these problems; however, these may or may not be appropriate and realistic for a given class or group of children. Some simpler games teachers can use to at least introduce these concepts. For example, solar energy can be explored by placing wet cloths in various places around the classroom — the sun's power as a drying agent will be easily established. Drying substances like fruit in a sunny spot will have the same effect.

Although the dangers of pollution do not readily lend themselves to conventional play, basic concepts can be introduced to children through play scenarios. These scenarios prepare students for more serious education in the higher grades. Children are very conscious of being preached to, however, so play scenarios should rely on simple playful concepts and not veer into strict instruction.

The early years' classroom environment builds the foundations for citizenship through the exploration and collaborative learning offered through playmaking. Children learn to see themselves as unique and valued contributors to the workings of the classroom community. Playmaking and exploration of everyday classroom problems help them to work together and understand that everyone has rights and responsibilities. An early introduction to the democratic processes at work in problem solving prepares young learners to embrace social responsibility and understanding of others and differing viewpoints. Although these concepts may be perceived as complex for the young learner, citizenship truly begins with the basics of taking turns, respecting others and their thoughts, understanding and feeling empathy for others, and choosing to become actively engaged.

Children's Books for Playful Learning

Books for drama and encouraging talk
- *Gingerbread Baby* by Jan Brett
- *Miss Nelson Is Missing* by Harry G. Allard (illustrated by James Marshall)
- *Barn Dance!* by Bill Martin, Jr. (illustrated by John Archambault)
- *The Doorbell Rang* by Pat Hutchins
- *Leonardo, the Terrible Monster* by Mo Willems
- Frog and Toad Books by Arnold Lobel
- *Alexander the Terrible, Horrible, No Good, Very Bad Day* by Judith Viorst
- *Aesop's Fables*, compiled by Lisbeth Zwerger

Books with humor
- *Look Out, Jack! The Giant Is Back!* by Tom Birdseye (illustrated by Will Hillenbrand)
- *Beware of the Storybook Wolves* by Lauren Child
- *Snow White in New York* by Fiona French
- *The Frog Prince Cont'd* by Jon Scieszka

Books that promote interacting with print knowledge
(how print is organized, vocabulary, meaning of words, role of words, directionality)
- *Each Peach Pear Plum* by Janet Ahlberg and Allan Ahlberg
- *The Very Busy Spider* by Eric Carle
- *Ten Potatoes in a Pot and Other Counting Rhymes* by Michael Jay Katz
- *Feathers for Lunch* by Lois Ehlert
- *Mama Cat Has Three Kittens* by Denise Fleming
- *Brown Bear, Brown Bear, What Do You See?* by Bill Martin, Jr. (illustrated by Eric Carle)
- *If You Give a Mouse a Cookie* by Laura Numeroff

Books that encourage narrative understanding
(that build understanding of the sequence of events, the characters and their actions, the setting of the story, the exciting part)
- *The Very Hungry Caterpillar* by Eric Carle (sequence of events)
- *Pete's a Pizza* by William Steig (interesting characters)
- *Diary of a Worm* by Doreen Cronin (setting)
- *Clifford's Birthday Party* by Norman Bridwell (high point of interest)
- *A Penguin Pup for Pinkerton* by Steven Kellogg (sequence of events)

- *The Snowy Day* by Ezra Jack Keats (setting)
- *My Truck Is Stuck!* by Kevin Lewis (illustrated by Daniel Kirk) (setting and environmental print)

Books that address identity
- *Giraffes Can't Dance* by Giles Andreae (illustrated by Guy Parker-Rees)
- *The Princesses Have a Ball* by Teresa Bateman (illustrated by Lynn Cravath)
- *Princess Smartypants* by Babette Cole
- *Prince Cinders* by Babette Cole
- *The Paper Bag Princess* by Robert Munsch (illustrated by Michael Martchenko)
- *Oliver Button Is a Sissy* by Tomie dePaola
- *The Sissy Duckling* by Harvey Fierstein (illustrated by Henry Cole)
- *Priscilla and the Pink Planet* by Nathaniel Hobbie (illustrated by Jocelyn Hobbie)
- *Jump* by Michelle Magorian (illustrated by Jan Ormerod)
- *The Boy Who Cried Fabulous* by Leslea Newman and Peter Ferguson
- *Who's in a Family?* by Robert Skutch (illustrated by Laura Nienhaus)
- *Pugdog* by Andrea U'Ren
- *No Two Snowflakes* by Sheree Fitch (illustrated by Janet Wilson)

Books that address individuality
- *Chester* by Melanie Watt
- *And Tango Makes Three* by Justin Richardson and Peter Parnell
- *Chrysanthemum* by Kevin Henkes
- *The Sound of Colors* by Jimmy Liao
- *Jackalope* by Janet Stevens
- *Groundhog Gets a Say* by Pamela Curtis Swallow (illustrated by Denise Brunkus)
- *The Dot* by Peter H. Reynolds
- *Olivia* by Ian Falconer
- *On the Day You Were Born* by Debra Frasier
- *All Dogs Have ADHD* by Kathy Hoopmann
- *Yo! Yes?* by Chris Raschka

Books that promote affirmation, imagination, appreciation of diversity
- *Elmer* by David McKee
- *Not a Box* by Antoinette Portis
- *Just Because I Am* by Lauren Murphy Payne (illustrated by Claudia Rohling)
- *One Hundred Is a Family* by Pam Ryan (illustrated by Benrei Huang)
- *Something from Nothing* by Phoebe Gilman
- *The Important Book* by Margaret Wise Brown
- *Skin Again* by bell hooks (illustrated by Chris Raschka)
- *The Family Book* by Todd Parr
- *The Name Jar* by Yangsook Choi
- *From Far Away* by Robert Munsch (illustrated by Michael Martchenko)
- *My Beautiful Child* by Lisa Desimini (illustrated by Matt Mahurin)
- *Papa's Latkes* by Michelle Edwards (illustrated by Stacey Schuett)
- *The Peace Book* by Todd Parr
- *David Gets in Trouble* by David Shannon
- *Treasure for Lunch* by Shanaa Nanji (illustrated by Yvonne Cathcart)

Books that encourage exploration of feelings

- *Grumpy Bird* by Jeremy Tankard
- *The Teddy Bear* by David McPhail
- *Scaredy Squirrel Makes a Friend* by Melanie Watt
- *Little Mouse's Big Book of Fears* by Emily Gravett
- *Chester's Way* by Kevin Henkes
- *When Sophie Gets Angry — Really, Really Angry . . .* by Molly Bang
- *How Smudge Came* by Nan Gregory (illustrated by Ron Lightburn)
- *Can't You Sleep, Little Bear?* by Martin Waddell (illustrated by Barbara Firth)
- *Stellaluna* by Janell Cannon
- *Feelings* by Aliki
- *All About You* by Catherine Anholt and Laurence Anholt
- *A Pocket Full of Kisses* by Audrey Penn (illustrated by Barbara Leonard Gibson)
- *Into My Mother's Arms* by Sharon Jennings (illustrated by Ruth Ohi)
- *Owl Babies* by Martin Waddell (illustrated by Patrick Benson)
- *The Kissing Hand* by Audrey Penn
- *Goggles!* by Ezra Jack Keats
- *Knuffle Bunny: A Cautionary Tale* by Mo Willems
- *My Friend Is Sad* by Mo Willems
- *Whoops! But It Wasn't Me* by Lauren Child
- *The Recess Queen* by Alexis O'Neill (illustrated by Laura Huliska-Beith)
- Franklin the Turtle Books by Paulette Bourgeois

Books that encourage play with patterning

- *Chicka Chicka 1, 2, 3* by Bill Martin, Jr., Michael Sampson, and Lois Ehlert
- *To Market, to Market* by Anne Miranda (illustrated by Janet Stevens)
- *Bear Wants More* by Karma Wilson (illustrated by Jane Chapman)
- *In the Tall, Tall Grass* by Denise Fleming
- *Polar Bear, Polar Bear, What Do You Hear?* by Bill Martin, Jr. (illustrated by Eric Carle)
- *What Game Shall We Play?* by Pat Hutchins
- *We're Going on a Bear Hunt* by Michael Rosen (illustrated by Helen Oxenbury)

Annotated Bibliography

Bowman, Barbara, and Evelyn K. Moore, eds. 2006. *School Readiness and Social-Emotional Development: Perspectives on Cultural Diversity*. Washington, DC: National Black Child Development Institute (NBCDI).

Among the 20–50 percent of children who enter Kindergarten not ready to learn, social-emotional development is often where they are least prepared. This collection of seven commissioned papers summarizes an NBCDI study of the current state of research and programs addressing preschoolers' social-emotional development. It identifies practical tools and strategies, as well as research, mental health screening, and community partnership models that can serve as resources for new research and program development.

Chaillé, Christine. 2007. *Constructivism across the Curriculum in Early Childhood Classrooms: Big Ideas as Inspiration*. Boston: Pearson Allyn and Bacon.

This book offers timely support for teachers who wish to bring constructivism and Reggio Emilia's ideas into their practice without losing sight of curriculum requirements. After providing a broad, theoretical framework, it discusses "Big Ideas," such as light, balance, cause and effect, transformation, sound, zooming in and out, and upside down as springboards for building an interdisciplinary, child-centred curriculum.

Chalufour, Ingrid, and Karen Worth. 2004. The Young Scientist Series from Redleaf Press.

See especially *Exploring Water with Young Children* (777), *Building Structures with Young Children* (748), and *Discovering Nature with Young Children* (758).

Colker, Laura J. 2005. *The Cooking Book: Fostering Young Children's Learning and Delight*. St. Paul, MN: Redleaf Press.

Cooking experiences give young children a chance to see a task through to completion and take pride in a product. As they prepare food, children learn social competence; science, math, and literacy skills; and the joy of creativity. Author Laura Colker has decades of experience cooking with children and teaching early childhood educators to do so.

Coply, Juanita V. 2000. *The Young Child and Mathematics*. New York: NAEYC/National Council of Teachers of Mathematics (NCTM).

This engaging, accessible book opens our eyes to young children's math interests and abilities. Consistent with both NAEYC guidelines on curriculum and assessment and the National Council of Teachers of Mathematics (NCTM)

Principles and Standards for School Mathematics, the book's lively vignettes and teacher-tested ideas will convert even those who proclaim, "I don't do math!"

Dragan, Pat. 2005. *A How-to Guide for Teaching English Language Learners in the Primary Classroom*. Portsmouth, NH: Heinemann.

In this wise and practical book, an experienced teacher outlines how to get non-native speakers started on language learning. She shares many innovative techniques and demonstrates how to build a classroom community that encourages and supports language learners by celebrating diversity, integrating language into all areas of the curriculum, and actively involving families. Written for Kindergarten to Grade 3 teachers, the book is also useful for teachers of younger children.

Epstein, Ann S. 2007. *The Intentional Teacher: Choosing the Best Strategies for Young Children's Learning*. Washington, DC: National Association for the Education of Young Children.

Intentional teachers keep in mind the key goals for children's learning and development in all domains by creating supportive environments, planning curriculum, and selecting from a variety of teaching strategies those that best promote each child's thinking and skills. *The Intentional Teacher* considers how and when each type of learning (child-guided, adult-guided, or a combination) is most effective, and what teachers can do to support them.

Jones, Elizabeth, Kathleen Evans, and Kay Stritzel Rencken. 2001. *The Lively Kindergarten: Emergent Curriculum in Action*. Washington, DC: National Association for the Education of Young Children.

Standards, accountability, and curriculum frameworks all have a place in education, but today's schools often push to the side what should be at the very centre: children and teachers. The result is classrooms that are less effective and immeasurably duller. Creating emergent curriculum is not easy, especially in the public-school world, but it is educationally powerful. Read eloquent stories of emergent curriculum in action — the struggles real teachers face and the strategies that make this approach work.

Gardner, Howard, David Henry Feldman, Mara Krechevsky, and Jie-Qi Chen, eds. 1998. *Project Spectrum: Early Learning Activities*. New York: Teachers College Press.

Howard Gardner's multiple-intelligences work has transformed our thinking about nurturing individual children's learning. From his innovative team comes this book of carefully developed learning activities in eight areas: mechanics and construction, science, music, math, visual arts, language, movement, and social understanding. This resource is the second volume of Project Zero Frameworks for Early Childhood Education.

Jones, Elizabeth, and John Nimmo. 1994. *Emergent Curriculum*. Washington, DC: National Association for the Education of Young Children.

The best curriculum isn't taken off the shelf or nailed down months before; it shifts and shapes to meet children's needs and interests, emerging as teachers and children interact with activities and lessons and weave their combined interests together. Listen in on the discussion among teachers in one program as they and their students move through the year with emergent curriculum. This stimulating resource will prompt both present and aspiring teachers to think about developing meaningful curriculum.

Kamii, Constance. 1982. *Number Is Preschool and Kindergarten: Educational Implications of Piaget's Theory*. Washington, DC: National Association for the Education of Young Children.

What arithmetic activities are better than teaching children to count and fill in worksheets? Hundreds! Children learn about numbers by voting, dividing snacks, playing games, even doing cleanup! Topics include the nature of number, objectives for teaching number, and principles of teaching.

Koralek, Derry, ed. 2005. *Spotlight on Young Children and the Creative Arts*. Washington, DC: National Association for the Education of Young Children.

The creative arts — music, movement, dramatic play, puppetry, painting, sculpture, and drawing, among them — are a crucial part of early childhood. Not only do they allow children to express themselves, but they can enhance development of their skills in literacy, science, math, social studies, and more. This engaging collection of articles includes resources and carefully designed questions and activities to aid teachers in reflecting on best practice.

Neugebauer, Bonnie, ed. 2007. *Play: A Beginnings Workshop Book*. Australia: Early Childhood Australia.

Top play experts discuss how play reflects and promotes development, how adults can support make-believe and block play, what the cultural dimensions of play are, and much more. This resource includes activities to do with children and personal anecdotes that will help caregivers better understand and support children's play.

Neuman, Susan, Kathleen Roskos, Tanya Wright, and Lisa Lenhart. 2007. *Nurturing Knowledge: Building a Foundation for School Success by Linking Early Literacy to Math, Science, Art and Social Studies*. New York: Scholastic.

This text presents five essential early literacy practices — creation of a supportive environment; shared book reading; songs, rhymes, and word play; developmental writing; and play — and provides the tools to link literacy to content knowledge in math, science, social studies, and art.

Riley, Dave, Robert San Juan, Joan Klinkner, and Ann Ramminger. 2008. *Social and Emotional Development: Connecting Science and Practice in Early Childhood Settings*. St. Paul, MN: Redleaf Press.

We know that holding babies while feeding them is important and that games such as Simon Says provide more than fun; however, we may not know why these practices in the social and emotional domains are so important for children's learning and development or how to explain our choices to others. With accessible language and numerous examples, this book examines the rationale and research base for best practices. Topics include attachment and exploration, friendship, impulse control, and problem-solving.

Rogers, Cosby, and Janet K. Sawyers. 1998. *Play in the Lives of Children*. Washington, DC: National Association for the Education of Young Children.

What is the best way for children to make the most of their lives? It's to engage in self-paced, child-controlled play! Find out why play is so important and how to support it in this convincing review of what we know about how children grow and learn. This book is comprehensive enough to serve as a textbook on play.

Schickedanz, Judith. 2008. *Increasing the Power of Instruction: Integration of Language, Literacy and Math across the Preschool Day*. Washington, DC: National Association for the Education of Young Children.

This accessible and wonderful book shows teachers how to maximize the scope and power of their instruction through integration across content domains and learning contexts. With a focus on language, literacy, and mathematics, Schickedanz introduces strategies that will bolster instruction in all subjects. Engaging vignettes demonstrate effective integration throughout the schedule, including during storytime, centre time, and large- and small-group sessions.

Seefeldt, Carol, and Alice Galper. 2005. *Active Experiences for Active Children: Social Studies.* 2d ed. Boston, MA: Prentice Hall.

This guide is full of theory, activities, planning ideas, and assessments to help plan and implement social studies curriculum for preschoolers and primary-grade students. It will be useful for anyone working with young children, from classroom teachers to childcare providers.

Strickland, Dorothy S., and Shannon Riley-Ayers. 2007. *Literacy Leadership in Early Childhood: The Essential Guide.* New York: Teachers College Press.

This resource covers key aspects of literacy learning and teaching, including child development, standards, curriculum planning, assessment, professional development, and connections between school and home. Attention is given throughout to issues related to linguistic and cultural diversity, and all chapters end with "leadership strategies" that serve as a quick guide for action and reflection.

Wien, Carol Anne, ed. 2008. *Emergent Curriculum in the Primary Classroom: Interpreting the Reggio Emilia Approach in Schools.* New York: Teachers College Press.

How is a compelling, exemplary curriculum created in schools in spite of the pressures to implement a standardized curriculum? In this book, teachers and principals share their experiences with emergent curriculum and with the creative practices they have developed in urban classrooms from Kindergarten to Grade 3. All contributors have found ways of interpreting the Reggio approach to enrich their teaching within the confines of traditional schools. This book is essential reading for anyone wishing to understand emergent curriculum and for all who hope to nurture an enlivening way to learn in classrooms.

Worth, Karen, and Sharon Grollman. 2003. *Worms, Shadows and Whirlpools.* Portsmouth, NH: Heinemann.

This book, inspired by Howard Gardner's recognition of the naturalist intelligence, makes a strong case for integrating science into the curriculum right from the start — creating a context for the development of language, mathematical thinking, and social skills. The book is filled with teacher stories, photographs, and examples of children's work, as well as commentary highlighting particular teaching strategies and child learning.

Wurm, Julianne. 2005. *Working in the Reggio Way.* St. Paul, MN: Redleaf Press.

Based on a U.S. teacher's first-hand experience observing and working in the schools of Reggio Emilia, Italy, this engaging book introduces the reflective, high-quality practices of the Reggio way. It emphasizes self-study and careful examination of teacher views of a child in order to bring the early childhood program into alignment with teacher values. The transformative book includes interactive activities for individual or group reflection.

References

Astington, J. W., & Baird, J. A. (Eds.). (2004). *Why language matters for theory of mind.* London: Oxford University Press.

Bandura, A. (1977). *Social learning theory.* Englewood Cliffs, NJ: Prentice-Hall.

Baroody, A. J., & Dowker, A. (Eds.). (2003). *The development of arithmetic concepts and skills: Constructing adaptive expertise.* Mahwah, NJ: Lawrence Erlbaum.

Barr, R. (2002). *Mother and child.* Millennium Dialogue on Early Child Development, November 12–14, 2001. Toronto: Atkinson Centre, OISE/UT.

Barton, D., & Hamilton, M. (2000). Literacy practices. In D. Barton, M. Hamilton, & R. Ivanic (Eds.), *Situated literacies: Reading and writing in context* (pp. 7–15). New York: Routledge.

Bernard, J., Freire, M., & Mulligan, V. (2004). *Canadian Parenting Workshops.* Toronto: Chestnut.

Branscombe, N. A., Castle, K., Dorsey, A. G., Surbeck, E., & Taylor, J. B. (2000). *Early childhood education — A constructivist approach.* Boston: Houghton Mifflin.

Brooker, L. (2002). *Starting school: Young children learning cultures.* Buckingham: Open University Press.

Bruner, J. (1978). The role of dialogue in language acquisition. In A. Sinclair, R. J. Jarvella, & W. J. M. Levelt (Eds.), *The child's conception of language* (pp. 241–55). New York: Springer-Verlag.

_____. (1990). *Acts of meaning.* Cambridge, MA: Harvard University Press.

Canadian Council on Learning (CCL). (2007). Survey of Canadian attitudes toward learning. Retrieved from http://www.ccl-cca.ca/CCL/Reports/SCAL/2007Archives

Canadian Language and Literacy Research Network. (2009). *National strategy for early literacy: Summary report* (Donald G. Jamieson). London, ON: Canadian Language and Literacy Research Network. Retrieved from http://www.cllrnet.ca/NSEL/summaryReport.pdf

Carr, M. (2001). A sociocultural approach to learning orientation in an early childhood setting. *Qualitative Studies in Education, 14*(4), 525–42.

Clark, M. (1996). *Young fluent readers.* London: Heinemann.

Cochran-Smith, M. (1984). *The making of a reader.* Norwood, NJ: Alblex.

Clay, M. M. (1991). *Becoming literate: The construction of inner control.* Portsmouth, NH: Heinemann Educational Books.

_____. (1993). *An observation survey of early literacy achievement.* Portsmouth, NH: Heinemann Educational Books.

Davidson, J., & Wright, J. (1994). The potential of the microcomputer in the early childhood classroom. In J. Wright & D. Shade (Eds.), *Young children: Active learners in a technological age.* Washington, DC: National Association for the Education of Young Children.

Dyson, A. H. (2003). *The brothers and sisters learn to write: Popular literacies in childhood and school cultures.* New York: Teachers College Press.

Edminston, B. (2007). Mission to Mars: Using drama to make a more inclusive classroom for literacy learning. *Language Arts, 84*(2): 337–46.

Elkind, D. (1981/1988/2001). *The hurried child.* Reading, MA: Addison-Wesley.

Erickson, E. (1963). *Childhood and society* (2nd ed.). New York: Norton.

Galda, L., Ash, G. E., & Cullinan, B. E. (2000). Research on children's literature. In M. L. Kamil, P. B. Mosenthal, P. D. Pearson, & R. Barr (Eds.), *Handbook of reading research* (Vol. 3). Mahwah, NJ: Lawrence Erlbaum.

Gardner, H. (1991). *Frames of mind.* New York: Basic Books.

_____. (2006). *Changing minds. The art and science of changing our own and other people's minds.* Boston, MA: Harvard Business School Press.

Graves, D. H. (1994). *A fresh look at writing.* Portsmouth, NH: Heinemann Educational Books.

Gregory, E., Long, S., & Volk D. (2005). A sociocultural approach to learning. In E. Gregory, S. Long, & D. Volk (Eds.), *Many pathways to literacy: Young children learning with siblings, grandparents, peers and communities.* New York: Routledge.

Griffiths, R. (2005). Mathematics and play. In Janet Moyles (Ed.), *The excellence of play* (2nd ed.). Buckingham, UK: Open University Press.

Hall, N. (1994). "Play, literacy and the role of the teacher." In J. Moyles (Ed.), *The excellence of play.* London: Paul Chapman.

_____. (1987). *The emergence of literacy.* Portsmouth, NH: Heinemann Educational Books.

_____. (2000). Literacy, play and authentic experience. In K. A. Roskos & J. F. Christie (Eds.), *Play and literacy in early childhood: Research from multiple perspectives* (pp. 189–204). Mahwah, NJ: Lawrence Erlbaum.

Harste, J. C., Burke, C. L., & Woodward, V. A. (1982). Children, their language and world: Initial encounters with print. In J. Langer & M. Smith-Burke (Eds.), *Reader meets author: Bridging the gap.* Newark, DE: International Reading Association.

Harste, J. C., Woodward, V. A., & Burke, C. L. (1984). *Language stories and literacy lessons.* Portsmouth, NH: Heinemann.

Heath, S. B. (1982). What no bedtime story means: Norwothine suiss at home on Shove. *Language and Society 11,* 49–75.

_____. (1983). *Ways with words: Language, life and work in communities.* New York: Cambridge University Press.

Hewes, J. (2007). *Let the children play: Nature's answer to early learning.* Montreal: Early Childhood Learning Knowledge Center.

Howe, A., & Davies, D. (2005). Science and play. In Janet Moyles (Ed.), *The excellence of play* (2nd ed.). Buckingham, UK: Open University Press.

Hughes, F. P. (1991). *Children play and development.* Needham, MA: Allyn & Bacon.

Kagan, S. (1998). *Examining children's readiness for school: Progress over the decade—A Report to the National Education Goals Panel.* Washington, DC: National Educational Goals Panel.

Kress, G. R. (2005). *Learning to write.* London: Taylor & Francis e-Library.

Marsh, J., & Hallett, E. (1999). *Desirable literacies: Approaches to language and literacy in the early years.* London: Paul Chapman.

Marsh, J., & Millard, E. (2000). *Literacy and popular culture: Using children's culture in the classroom.* London: Paul Chapman.

Miller, E., & Almon, J. (2009). *Crisis in the Kindergarten: Why children need to play in school.* College Park, MD: Alliance for Childhood. Retrieved from Alliance for Childhood website: http://www.allianceforchildhood.org.

Milne, R. (1997). *Marketing play.* Melbourne, AU: Free Kindergarten Association.

Moll, L., Amanti, C., Neff, D., & Gonzales, N. (1992). Funds of knowledge for teaching: Using a qualitative approach to connect homes and classrooms. *Theory into Practice, 31*(2): 132–41.

Morrow, L. M., & Rand, M. K. (1991). Promoting literacy during play by designing early childhood classroom environments. *The Reading Teacher, 44*(6): 396–402.

Morrow, L. M., Strickland, D. S., & Wood, D. G. (1998). *Literacy instruction in half- and whole-day Kindergarten.* Newark, NJ: International Reading Association.

Mustard, J. F. (2006). *Early child development and experience-based brain development: The scientific underpinnings of the importance of early childhood development in a globalized world.* Washington, DC: Brookings Institution.

National Head Start Association [website]. http://www.nhsa.org/.

Nemoianu, A. M. (1980). *The boat's gonna leave: A study of children learning a second language from conversations with other children.* Amsterdam: John Benjamins.

Newman, S., & Dickinson, D. (2001). *Handbook of early literacy research.* New York: Guilford Press.

Ontario Ministry of Education. (2006). *Kindergarten program.* Toronto: Government of Ontario.

Parr, T. (2003). *The family book.* New York: Little, Brown Young Readers.

Pascal, C. (2004). *Education in childcare and childcare in education: What are the challenges and benefits?* Presentation at the European Conference on Childcare in a Changing World, Groningen, the Netherlands, October 21–23.

_____. (2009). *With our best future in mind: Implementing early learning in Ontario.* Report to the Premier by the Special Advisor on Early Learning.

Pelletier, J. (2006). *Parent involvement: Best Start Expert Panel of Early Learning Workshops.* Toronto: Ministry of Children and Youth Services.

Pelligrini, A. D. (1991). *Applied child study: A developmental approach.* Mahwah, NJ: Lawrence Erlbaum.

Piaget, J. (1962). *Play, dreams, and imitation in childhood.* New York: Norton.

Piper, T. (2003). *Language and learning: The home and school years* (3rd ed.). Upper Saddle River, NJ: Merrill.

Rosenblatt, L. M. (1978). *The reader, the text, the poem: The transactional theory of the literacy work.* Carbondale, IL: Southern Illinois University Press.

Roskos, K., & Christie, J. (Eds.). (2000). *Play and literacy in early childhood: Research from multiple perspectives.* Mahwah, NJ: Lawrence Erlbaum.

Roskos, K., & Christie, J. (2004). Examining the play literacy interface: A critical review and future directions. In E. Ziegler, D. Singer, & J. Bishop (Eds.), *Child's play: The roots of reading* (pp. 95–124). Washington, DC: Zero to Three Press.

Rubin, K. H., Fein, H. G., & Vandenberg, B. (1983). Play. In E. M. Hetherington (Vol. Ed.), *Handbook of child psychology: Vol 4. Social development* (4th ed.). New York: Wiley.

Saracho, O. (1991). The role of play in early childhood curriculum. In B. Spodek & O. Saracho (Eds.), *Issues in early childhood curriculum.* New York: Teachers College Press.

Schrader, C. (1990). Symbolic play as a curricular tool for early literacy development. *Early Childhood Research Quarterly, 5,* 79–103.

Siraj-Blatchford, I., & Clarke, P. (2000). *Supporting identity, diversity, and language in the early years.* Buckingham, UK: Open University Press.

Smilansky, S. (1968). *The effects of sociodramatic play on disadvantaged preschool children.* New York: Wiley.

_____. (1990). Socio-dramatic play: Its relevance to behavior and achievement in school. In E. Klugman & S. Smilansky (Eds.), *Children's play and learning: Perspectives and policy implications.* New York: Teachers College Press.

Sulzby, E. (1985). Children's emergent reading of favorite storybooks: A developmental study. *Reading Research Quarterly, 20,* 458–81.

_____, Teale, W. H., & Kamberelis, G. (1989). Emergent writing in the classroom: Home and school connections. In D. S. Strickland & L. M. Morrow (Eds.), *Emerging literacy: Young children learn to read and write* (pp. 147–59). Newark, DE: International Reading Association.

Street, B. (Ed.). (2000). Literacy events and literacy practices. In M. Martin-Jones & K. Jones (Eds.), *Multilingual literacies.* Amsterdam: John Benjamins.

Sutton-Smith, B. (1971). The playful modes of knowing. In N. Curry & S. Arnaud (Coordinators), *Play: The child strives toward self-realization* (pp. 13–24). Conference proceedings of the National Association for the Education of Young Children. Washington, DC.

Teale, W. H., & Sulzby, E. (Eds.). (1986). *Emergent literacy: Writing and reading* (Vol. 6 in Writing Research Series). Norwood, NJ: Alblex.

Vygotsky, L. S. (1934/1986). *Thought and language.* Cambridge, MA: MIT Press.

Wells, G. (1999). *Dialogic inquiry: Towards a sociocultural practice and theory of education.* New York: Cambridge University Press.

Wenger, E. (1998). *Communities of practice: Learning, meaning, and identity.* Cambridge: Cambridge University Press.

Wong, Lily Fillmore. (1976). *The second time around: Cognitive and social strategies in second language acquisition.* (Unpublished doctoral dissertation). Palo Alto, CA: Stanford University.

Acknowledgments

Many thanks to . . .
- the inspiring playmaking teachers Carol, Karen, Laura, Trevor, Liz, Leslie, Jenny, Susan, Nancy, Debbie, Nina, Kelly, Julia, Shawna, Christine, Carrie, Sue Ann, and Mernia, who have nurtured the wonderful imaginations of the children we teach;
- the schools that still value play as a form of learning; and
- the adventurous players who met me on the playground . . . the princesses and princes and frightening dragons . . . the superhero team who saved me from the bad guys.

Thanks also go to
- my classroom research assistants, Julia, Chandra, and Cheryl, and
- these researchers and advocates of play: Joyce Bainbridge, Linda Cameron, Toni Doyle, Tara-Lynn Scheffel, Roz Stooke, and Janette Hughes.

I thank my mentor, David Booth, for his playful thoughtfulness and attentive foreword; Kate Revington, for her conscientious editing; and Mary Macchiusi, for seeing the value in sharing the classroom-based research represented in this resource and the voices of some who see play as the important work that children do.

And, of course, I give thanks to . . .
Bob and Aidan — playmakers extraordinaire.

Index